Male Pattern Behaviour
The annotated journals of Thomas Furphy

Portrait of Señora Sabasa Garcia
Frederico de Goya
National Gallery of Art, USA
Andrew W. Mellon collection

The portrait of Señora Sabasa Garcia
An appreciation by Thomas Furphy

Goya's portrait of Sabasa Garcia was painted when Goya was squarely in the middle of his most productive and assured period as a portrait artist. It displays all the characteristics of the best works of this time: the astonishing technique; the depiction of detail in a few, rapid brushstrokes; the absence of distracting background; the restricted colour palette. It differs from almost all others in one, possibly apocryphal, detail: Goya chose this subject.

Commissioned to paint the portrait of Evaristo Pérez de Castro, then Spain's minister of foreign affairs, legend has it that Sabasa Garcia, the minister's niece, visited her uncle after Goya had begun work. Goya was so struck with her beauty, he immediately stopped work on the commission and asked permission to paint her portrait.

We know little about the life of Sabasa Garcia. At the time of the portrait, she was sixteen and recently married. She kept the portrait until her death.

Critics usually focus on the astonishing virtuosity of Goya's brushwork. The gold of Sabasa's shawl shimmers with light. Her mantilla is a transparent film, a delicate gossamer of lace framing the beauty of her face.

Viewers of the painting who are not critics rarely notice the brushwork. They concentrate only on the girl: the radiant beauty of the face, the soft lips, the dark eyes, and the expression that cannot be read as a single meaning. She looks out at the viewer with a deep sadness, perhaps fearful or hurt, but strong, brave, intelligent.

She is a woman who is facing her future in the knowledge that there is no safety in the world but her own resolve.

Male Pattern Behaviour

Male Pattern Behaviour

The annotated journals of Thomas Furphy

Howard Firkin

In Case Of Emergency Press

http://www.icoe.com.au
Travancore, Victoria
Australia

Published by In Case of Emergency Press 2018

Copyright © Howard Firkin

The right of Howard Firkin to be identified as the author of this work has been asserted by him in accordance with the Copyright, Designs and Patents Act, 1988, despite initial and strenuous denials.

ISBN 978-0-9943525-0-7

Wer jetzt kein Haus hat, baut sich keines mehr.
Wer jetzt allein ist, wird es lange bleiben,
wird wachen, lesen, lange Briefe schreiben
und wird in den Alleen hin und her
unruhig wandern, wenn die Blätter treiben.

Aus *'Herbsttag'* von **Rainer Maria Rilke**

Table of contents

Something that isn't a medical condition	1
Some background becomes foreground	20
The plot to beard Bluebeard	36
Weekend Execution	49
Success and stress	59
An extended breather	74
Farewell and a chance to say hello	79
Catalogue of disgust	88
The best form of defence	98
A little spot of housework; a little bit of history	109
More housework; more history	127
Postcard	137
Dr No's student days	141
Love is declared	148
So this is how it feels	155
Return	162
Doctor No says... nothing much	167
Metamorphosis	174
Adelaide	176
Epilogue	182

Something that isn't a medical condition

> Awoke without an erection again. This is the seventh day in a row. Enough is enough.

Two things strike me when I read this short entry: the essential male desire to *do something*; and the disproportionate influence that the arbitrary has on male decision-making. There is no hint in that entry that the appropriate response might be to examine the situation in a thoughtful way. Thought is seldom the first weapon we reach for. Why is enough enough after seven days, not six, or five, or nine? You know why: because seven days make a week; so enough is enough because of the chance that we have chosen to bundle days into something we call weeks which we have arbitrarily decided should contain seven days. For no reason at all, one of these 'weeks' is long enough to endure not waking with an erection.

Men like to *do*. And we *do* without reason. This is a part, an important part, of male pattern behaviour.

Doing something in this case involved making an appointment to see a doctor. My regular doctor, a Malaysian Chinese whose surname is No and who models his bedside manner on the Bond villain of the same name, was unlikely to be sympathetic. He would take my blood pressure, weigh me, give me the usual admonitions, and then ask, "What do you expect? You are no longer a young man. What do you want with erections? They are only trouble. Take up golf." And then he would charge me for a physical check-up and an hour's counselling.

Don't misunderstand. I respect Dr No. He is my go-to health professional when I need to excuse myself from something or make light of a serious symptom, but he would treat my erection concerns as if they were his own: he would ignore them. At best, he might prescribe Viagra or Cialis or something similar. "You want an erection? This will give you an erection. You work out what to do with it."

I knew him too well. "You think it will make you happy? Dr No knows. Dr No says 'No!' You listen to Dr No."

Dr No has a single prescription for me: "You need to work. Sitting on your arse all day will kill you. And no one will notice! You need to work so people miss you when you die."

People will miss Dr No.

So, the search had to begin for a new doctor. No one in my current suburb. Google to the rescue. 'Medical practice sexual dysfunction city centre' revealed the less than surprising information that Melbourne was awash with sexual problems and with a variety of professionals willing to treat them. Apex Medical Centre looked suitably anonymous. I called them to make an appointment and discovered they had a vacancy in three days' time if I preferred regular business hours, or I could see one of their after-hours doctors that evening at 8:30.

Perfect.

There was an extra charge for the after-hours consultations: a $55- security fee.

Not a problem. I crave security. See you at 8:30.

I now had the whole day to work on my latest project: A Programme for Moderate Political Reform in Australia.

The Programme was something I had been exploring for some time. My interest was sporadically triggered by events in the political world which excited me to return to the creation of a cohesive programme of reform. Today's trigger was the excitement generated by proposed changes to the way people vote to elect the Federal Senate. As usual, politicians were reviewing these changes through the distorting lens of self-interest. Hardly a surprise when the need for the proposed changes was only visible when viewed through the same device, but like the disappearance of my mornings' erectile powers, apparently the time had come to do something. Enough was enough.

I made use of the morning to register a website for the Programme—*www.pmpra.com*—and to fashion a short placeholder page for what would become my blog. The afternoon was given over to writing a portion of the Programme. The idea was to write an article each week and publish it on the blog, and then collect the entries together in a single volume and publish the Programme to general acclaim.

You may say I'm a dreamer, but I'm not the only one. Just the only one interested in moderate political reform in Australia. But all that would change. Eventually, not even I would be interested.

*

What use are political parties?

Extract from A Programme of Moderate Political Reform in Australia, www.pmpra.com

Political parties have been around for so long that seldom does anyone stop to ask, 'What is their purpose? Why do we have political parties?' and more importantly, perhaps, 'Do we need political parties?'

I suggest that, not only do political parties serve no constructive purpose, they are actively inimical to democracy and we should outlaw them altogether.

Political parties in Western democracies, are generally agreed to spring from the Petitioners and Abhorrers (later, by adoption of the derogatory terms that opponents used to belittle them, they became known as Whigs and Tories) of seventeenth century England. And it's all been downhill from there.

The cheery website of the Parliamentary Education Office ('Educating Schools, Students and Teachers about Parliament') pushes the line that political parties aim 'to have members elected to Parliament so their ideas can affect the way Australia is governed', which is rather like describing a pederast as someone who 'cherishes time spent with young people and enjoys introducing them to new ideas and practices'.

Political parties are piratical bands, united only by self-interest, which aim to have members elected to Parliament to protect and further the interests of the pirates. All political parties seek to make the common wealth of the Commonwealth less common and more particular.

The objection might be raised that some parties—especially the so-called 'single issue' parties—are not seeking large scale redistribution of wealth but are only concerned to have a particular concern addressed, but this is a naïve objection. All political parties start life as single issue parties. There is always one underlying, fundamental issue or concern used to amass support. The reason is simple: you cannot chant a manifesto. Once a political party has its slogan, has its single issue audience, those who lead the party expand its policies to cover the entire range of their self-interest. Its supporters, whose only concern is the single issue they have rallied behind, continue to support the party because they continue to identify themselves with that single issue.

Political parties only sprang into existence at a time when parliamentary democracy was a pale and weakly bairn. Conditions have changed. We live in a society with a literate and informed population which has an expectation of having their voices heard, and there are ever more, and ever more effective, means of individuals expressing their opinions. Allowing formal aggregations into political parties can only stifle variety of opinion. How does that assist democracy?

People sometimes make the argument that voters 'prefer to vote for their parties, not knowing the individual candidates'. This is a hardly a reason to keep them. It is, on the contrary, a powerful reason to do away with them! Reducing a complex decision to a choice between two or three poorly understood alternatives may make it easier to make a decision, but it does nothing to ensure one makes the right decision.

© Copyright 2016, Thom Furphy

*

In the evening I headed into the city for my appointment at Apex Medical Centre. The address was on Collins Street, a modest eight storeyed building, built in the twenties or thirties and refurbished in the early seventies to obliterate any potential charm or architectural interest. Whoever the current owners of the building were, they were remaining doggedly true to that 1970's strategy. Apex Medical Centre was the only business listed on the third floor. I entered an Otis Elevator and was greeted with a muzak version of 'Dock of the bay'; I was unclear about the message the cosmos was sending me. On the third floor, I ceased restin' my bones, left the elevator, and pushed open a glass door, sandblasted with the name Apex. It looked original, as though it had once been the front door of a long-failed trading company. I wondered if the practice had been named to save the expense of a new door.

Expecting a bored receptionist to be seated behind a blond wood desk, I was surprised to see a bored, young woman sitting behind a blond wood desk. Surprised, because standing beside her, holding a folder of case notes, was Dr No.

"Welcome, Mr Furphy!" exclaimed Dr No.

"Good," I managed to burble. Perhaps I thought he was asking me how I was. I recovered quickly, however. "I was hoping I'd get you."

"Come through, come through."

He led the way to a small consulting room: desk, doctor's chair, two patients' chairs, examination couch, medical paraphernalia.

"Now, what can I do for you, Mr Furphy?"

The question looks bland on the page, but it was seasoned with a complex Chinese Malay spice mix of betrayed professional trust.

"I have an embarrassing problem, Dr No. I didn't want to see you at the practice…"

"You knew I worked here?" Dr No asked, trying not to sound like the Chinese detective in a bad film of a thirties novel.

I made that up. He probably had no idea that he might sound like a Chinese detective in a bad film of a thirties novel. He certainly wouldn't have cared.

"No," I answered truthfully, and then left the truth where it couldn't hurt anybody, "but I asked who the doctors were when I rang and I was hoping there was only one Dr No."

"Oh. Lucky day for both of us," he finished, sourly. "Now, what's this problem so embarrassing you have to come into the city and make me pay 30% of my fee to Apex?"

"Erections."

"Too many? Not enough?"

"Not enough."

"Mornings?"

"Gone missing."

"What do you expect? You are no longer a young man. What do you want with erections? They are only trouble. Take up golf."

I told you I could have written it. But then came the second Dr No-related surprise of the evening.

"You think I'm going to write you a prescription for Viagra, Cialis?"

"Oh, I… I hadn't thought of it," I lied.

"Everyone's a doctor. You think you're a doctor? Why aren't you working sixty hours a week if you're a doctor?"

"Because I'm not a doctor."

"That's right. Dr No is a doctor. Are you a doctor? Dr No says 'No!' You listen to Dr No."

I have only ever had one consultation with him where Dr No has been unable to work in his 'Dr No says No' routine.

Something that isn't a medical condition

"You need to work. Sitting on your arse all day will kill you. And no one will notice! You need to work so people miss you when you die. And in the meantime, sticky tape test."

I thought I'd misheard him.

"What sort of test?"

"Sticky tape. You can use a postage stamp, too, but sticky tape is cheaper. Before bye-byes you wrap a small collar of paper or plastic wrap around your penis. You fasten it with a tiny piece of sticky tape. Just enough to hold it in place. Then you go to sleep. No self-pleasure on test night, please!"

"Why am I gift wrapping my penis?"

"If the penis collar is still in place in the morning, we know you haven't had an erection in the night. If the collar is broken, your penis has become erect in the night or early morning and we know that your lack of erections — reported lack of erections —" he added pointedly, "is psychological. Usual in these cases and almost certain for you. Roll up your sleeve."

"You know my blood pressure is fine."

"Not in this practice, I don't. Blood pressure is part of the male wellness check-up. Only $70–. Worth it for you."

After my wellness check-up, which surprisingly involved no further physical examination — "Your prostate is fine without me annoying it." — Dr No told me to make another appointment in a day or two so I could report on the sticky tape test.

"I will write a letter to your GP suggesting he contact you to arrange a couple of follow up appointments to check on your progress."

Dr No was going to make sure he recovered his 30%.

I left his consulting room and went to reception to pay and to make a follow up appointment. Only as I approached the desk did I notice that the bored, young woman was beautiful. I was searching about for a clever line to spin when the voice of Dr

Something that isn't a medical condition

No spilled out of the office, "Sticky tape test for Mr Furphy! Appointment for two days' time."

The bored receptionist made eye contact with me for long enough to ensure I displayed my discomfort and understanding of her complete disdain, and then she made another evening appointment for two days' time. I went home, stopping at a convenience store to buy some sticky tape.

*

> Awoke to the double humiliation of no erection and a broken penis collar. My condition is not medical but psychosomatic. Why isn't psychosomatic medical? Isn't the brain part of the body? And shouldn't I write 'triple' humiliation? What could be more humiliating that having fashioned and worn a penis collar?

Clearly, I was not in the mood for writing that morning. The ideas I was exploring then interest me now. Why didn't they interest me on that morning? Why do we regard the psychosomatic as outside bodily health? Pain is pain and is only pain if it registers as pain in the brain, which, incidentally, sits atop and within the body. If a condition is psychosomatic and causes pain or discomfort or dysfunction, why is that different from a viral condition which exhibits the same symptoms? Isn't every symptom of pain psychosomatic?

Perhaps I wasn't interested because those ideas aren't all that interesting.

Forgetting the psychosomatic for the moment, another word jumps out of that entry: humiliation. This is a very male preoccupation. A baffling one in many ways. Imagine if you tried to define for an alien race the ways in which human males can suffer humiliation and tried to make sense of it for them. A man might be humiliated by a woman rejecting him, accepting him, rejecting another, accepting another, smiling, not smiling, talking, not talking, walking away, not moving, saying something, saying nothing. In short, a man can rightly feel humiliated by anything and heaven help anyone (particularly a

Something that isn't a medical condition

woman) who doesn't understand that. Heaven help the alien if it's smaller and harmless. The armour-shelled alien with razored claws and nine inch canine teeth is probably safe.

Why did I feel humiliated? Let's list the ways I was humiliated that I noted in that journal entry:

1. I felt humiliated because I woke with no erection
2. I felt humiliated because the broken paper penis collar suggested that I had had an erection, but that it had fled before the return of consciousness
3. I felt humiliated because I had a 'psychosomatic condition'
4. I felt humiliated because, apparently, it is unworthy of a man to spend a few minutes fashioning a paper collar for his penis and then spending a few moments next morning examining its condition

So not a triple humiliation, but the rare quad humiliation. There might be a spot for me in the Olympics if I stuck to my training schedule.

Why is/was it important to me to wake with an erection? Is the morning erection so much a part of the male image of self that to wake without an erection is somehow emasculating? What do you do with an erection, anyway?

You may imagine you know the answer to that last question, but not having a partner who wished to have it inserted, withdrawn, inserted, etc. and having largely outgrown the desire to pump it myself while imagining it being inserted, withdrawn, inserted, etc. into a woman whom I would never meet, the answer is not as obvious as it might seem. Why shouldn't I simply spring out of bed, perform my set of sprightly callisthenic exercises and get on with the day? Why should I fret?

On this particular day, I remember having no answer to those questions; so I sprang out of bed, convinced myself I had forgotten the callisthenic exercises, and headed to the toilet to empty my bladder. As the last sporadic streams of pale urine left on their long adventure, I shook my penis vigorously, imagining this might have some callisthenic benefit and then paused, shook again, paused, rubbed gently, paused… nothing. Whatever genie still lurked in that bottle, it wasn't making an appearance this morning.

I set myself the task of documenting the importance of the erection to the male psyche.

*

The importance of the erection

Extract from the unpublished work, 'Masculinear', by Thomas Furphy

The erection has a biological importance. Despite the theories of seers like William Chidley, the erection is likely to have contributed so much to the successful and continuing reproduction of our species that it may be regarded as essential to humanity. We can argue about 'essential' if you like, but let's not. The male with the rock hard erection is more likely to reproduce successfully than the gent with the semi-tumescent sea-slug. No doubt, said gent could shoehorn his flaccid member into some particularly accommodating (or unconscious) woman and perhaps even achieve ejaculation, but it's always going to be easier with a stiffie.

Even so, does this explain the whole importance of the erection to the masculine mind?

It might be argued that few men are thinking of the likelihood of successful insemination while they are engaged in their various erection-wrangling pursuits. Indeed, many chaps engage in activities in which impregnation is a very unlikely outcome, no matter how impressive their erections or how diligently and imaginatively they apply them in their undertakings. If they aren't thinking of reproduction, what then is the importance of the erection?

Pleasure, obviously. It is more enjoyable (I speak from experience) to engage in sexual activities with an erection than without one. But while it's nice to have a shag an' all, if you are unable to have one, what are you missing? What you are missing is what you cannot have: in other words, nothing that can be missed because it isn't possible. You might *want* it, but you can't *miss* it. And presumably,

Something that isn't a medical condition

you can devote yourself to other pursuits, uninterrupted by the need to employ an erection.

And yet, the erection is important to the male mind. I contend that it is—for most men—central to their idea of the male role. The male role includes erections. Erections, what's more, on demand. It is not enough to be able to command the appearance of an impressive erection once a month, for example. The male mind requires that the erection should be able to be conjured up at will. And while there are certain unwritten rules regarding when it is acceptable to be unable to command the member to attention, these are restricted to time limits after serious rogering, or moments of great peril.

The result is that the male self-image is hostage to the erection.

© Copyright 2016, Thom Furphy

*

When I re-read that passage from *'Masculinear'*, knowing its genesis, I don't know that I have actually captured the real angst of my then situation. My self-image may have been hostage to the erection, but I had received no demands, no indication from the kidnapper that the hostage was safe and able to be released on payment of whatever enormous sum.

What did erection want from me to free me again?

More men need to ask themselves this question. What does erection want from me? In the coming weeks, I would discover that what erection wanted from me was a complete breakdown, a total negation of self, a wracking self-doubt and total spiritual and mental impoverishment.

Erection would require me to fall in love.

No one deserves that.

*

Something that isn't a medical condition

> Evening. Toying with the idea of repeating the penis collar experiment. Because it's a Wednesday night and Spanish movie night on SBS, I am likely to fall asleep on the couch; so I should create the penis collar and wear it while I'm watching the television. I have found a pretty Japanese serviette which is tissue and has a pattern of flying swallows. I will tear off a small strip, create the collar and settle down to enjoy the Spanish genius for imagining plausible occasions for beautiful young women to expose their breasts.

What the final entry in February fails to mention is that barely an hour into watching a particularly baffling Spanish police drama where the beautiful female detective was interrupted in the shower and answered her apartment intercom naked and dripping and was clearly about to open the door to the beautiful but dangerous female suspect who was going to try to seduce her, there was a knock on my own door. I was not naked and dripping, but I was wearing only a small, nylon happy coat Norma had bought on her 1974 holiday cruise and wearing a Japanese tissue penis collar (not visible through the happy coat).

Just ignore it, you might say. Perhaps they'll go away, not guessing the occupant is awake. But I had the television turned up quite loud because I was trying to learn Spanish. I like their approach to breasts. Besides, a visitor was not a common occurrence for me. As rare as erections at that point in my life.

I went to the front door, checked the happy coat didn't reveal anything too happy, and opened the door. A burst of Spanish from the television introduced a beautiful Spanish woman into my life.

"May I come in, please?" she asked, urgently. She was small and had thick dark hair.

"You're Spanish? Your accent is barely noticeable."

The small, dark woman pushed past me and shut the door.

Something that isn't a medical condition

"No, I'm not Spanish. I need to make a phone call."

"In English?"

I don't know why I asked it. She had turned to face me and she was stunningly beautiful. I'm not always coherent when confronted by exceptional beauty.

Memo: the male mind can be extremely fast. Having registered that a beautiful woman was in my house, I was already planning ways I could discreetly dispose of the penis collar without her knowing.

"Phone?" she asked, brusquely.

"Sorry, I should have anticipated your arrival and had it ready for you." I answered, in a dignified but hurt tone, drawing my happy coat around me to ensure no glimpse of the penis collar. Dignity was something else I'd have to explore in *'Masculinear'*.

"I'm sorry," she replied, without a trace of sorrow in her voice, "I'm in a hurry. A violent man is looking for me and I need to be elsewhere. Phone?"

At the same moment, we heard a car door slam outside. Her face changed from expressing irritation with an obtuse man to terror at the sound of a violent one.

"Go into the bedroom. Don't make a noise. Wait," I instructed her.

She didn't hesitate. She dashed into the room I had pointed to and stood behind the door. I scurried into the kitchen and grabbed the rubbish bag out of the kitchen bin and opened the front door.

"What are you doing?" I heard her hiss.

"Stay there!" I hissed back, as if I had some idea what I was doing.

I walked out into the night, holding the happy coat together with one hand, the bag of garbage in the other. As I walked towards the front gate a dark gorilla shape loomed on the other side of the fence.

Something that isn't a medical condition

"Can I help you?" I asked, querulously.

"Have you seen a woman? I need to get her to hospital," the gorilla explained with breathless hurry or homicidal fury.

"Someone ran past a moment ago," I ventured helpfully. "That way," I pointed, releasing the happy coat and displaying a flaccid member swaddled in Japanese tissue.

The gorilla ran off along the road in the direction my finger indicated and my penis didn't. I placed the garbage bag in the rubbish bin, collected my happy coat about me again, and watched him for a moment: about my build, but with the upper body definition of a man who worked out at a gym. I headed back into the house, rehearsing the only Spanish phrase I knew with certainty: "Sus pechos son como los melocotones de verano"; your breasts are like summer-ripe peaches.

*

> Conversation is no substitute for sex.

Another brief entry which does not reveal the pain which is father to the observation. I re-entered my house to find my visitor peering around the bedroom door.

I closed the door, master of the situation.

"Has he gone?" she asked, peering around the door.

"Apparently so."

The woman started moving towards the front door.

"I'd better go then. Thanks for that."

Male brain, male brain, male brain!

"I don't think that's a good idea." Think, think, think! "He can't be far yet." Brilliant! "I sent him off in one direction, but when he doesn't find you, he'll return to his car. The safest thing we can do is wait until we hear the car drive off."

She stopped, hand on the door knob.

"You're right. I'll stay here for a while."

Interesting twist: the male brain, still congratulating itself for cunningly manoeuvring a beautiful woman into staying, was offended that she should presume she could.

"Go into the living room. Watch the tele. I'll make tea or would you prefer coffee?"

"Nothing thanks. I need to get going."

"Of course. Into the living room. Keep the tele on so it sounds like I'm some sort of lonely no-hoper who isn't entertaining anyone, and I'll make myself some tea."

"Okay. Good idea. White with none. Coffee."

The male brain had concluded its congratulations and was exploring offended in more detail. Coffee it would be. As instant as it comes: No Name Instant Coffee; No Name non-dairy whitener. Presumptuous Spanish bitch. On reaching the kitchen, however, the summer-ripe peaches intervened and I took out the Melbourne Grind coffee and switched on the espresso machine. And made myself a pot of Sri Lankan tea. That would show her.

I fussed about with the tea and coffee and may have looked for a biscuit. The weevils had beaten me to the No Name Golden Wheat Biscuits; so I restricted the tray to milk and sugar. I carried the tray into the living room and saw my guest sitting nervously on the edge of a chair. The television burbled its way through the knotted Spanish plot, but she paid it no attention. She smiled weakly as I put down the tray. At least she's trying, I thought.

"Your coat is open." She remarked quietly while concentrating with exaggerated care on her coffee.

I hastily pulled it shut and sat opposite, crossing my legs carefully. I was too far away from my tea to reach it, and I wasn't going to stand again in a hurry.

"So, while we're snowed in here, perhaps we can entertain each other with the stories of our lives and how we ended up here?"

"Nothing to tell. I am involved with a man who is violent. I can extract myself and I will. Have. As soon as the car is gone I will leave you in peace. But thank you for your trouble."

"You have lightened an otherwise dreary evening." Light-hearted. Debonair. Devil-may-care man-of-the-world. So many hyphens. "You should perhaps think through your escape strategy, however."

She turned an angry, suspicious look on me.

"What do you mean?"

"Why don't you tell me what you're planning? I'm a chance acquaintance; you never have to see me again. Perhaps I can offer some advice, even some help."

"You did well with the rubbish bag," she muttered, half to herself. "Okay. I have a sister in Sydney. I'm going there. I've left everything behind, but I don't care. I can replace anything he's got."

"Won't he look there?"

"What can he do?"

"You tell me, but you don't flit to Sydney to escape a man who likes Morris dancing," I answered glibly and probably wrongly. I'd certainly travel to Sydney to avoid Morris dancing.

"I can't stay in Melbourne. He's dangerous."

Ah, male brain, wouldn't this have been a good time to drink your tea and offer to call the woman a cab?

"Only dangerous if he knows where you are. Stay in Melbourne where he doesn't know where you are and lie low for a little while. He's almost certain to get in touch with your sister and stake her out if he thinks you're there. There's nothing to connect you to here."

"Except this is the last place he saw me!"

Something that isn't a medical condition

"He's never seen you here. He's seen me. So what? We've never met. None of your friends can inadvertently mention this place."

"What's your name?" she asked me abruptly.

"Thom. Thom Furphy."

"Well, listen, Tom-tom Furphy, I've just escaped one lunatic, controlling male. Whatever you're thinking, forget it. I'm not getting involved with another."

"That's right," I agreed, indicating the man sitting before a cooling pot of Sri Lankan tea, "you'd be getting involved with a civilised man who happens to have the necessary resources — roof, room, income — to share with a fellow mortal for as short or long a time as suits us both. You can't think I look terribly threatening, surely."

"Men never do, at first."

"Your choice, of course, but whatever you decide, unless you have a better plan, come with me and let me show you to a room where you can at least be comfortable and safe tonight."

I led her down the small corridor to Norma's room — the main bedroom of the house — and showed her inside. Norma's room is decorated in a charmingly old-fashioned manner. The wallpaper is a gentle yellow with small floral devices floating all over it. The polished boards are mostly covered with a large rug of Persian design and Indian origin which is almost new (for good reason). The bed is an old double bed of dark wood, but the mattress is new (same good reason) and I keep the bed made up with good quality bed linen in case I should ever have guests.

"The window is fly-screened if you'd like it open. It shouldn't be too musty; I vacuum every fortnight. The bathroom is further down the hall. I sleep in the second bedroom opposite the bathroom. Even if I snore, I shouldn't disturb you. There are spare night things in the drawers there. I'll leave you to have a look around, and make yourself comfortable while I

Something that isn't a medical condition

make a couple of sandwiches. If you still want to risk flight, I'll call you a cab."

"There's no key in the lock."

I wasn't sure I'd heard her correctly. "Sorry?"

She pointed to the keyhole below the porcelain door knob.

"There's a lock, but no key."

I wasn't sure what point she was making. "There's never been a key as far as I know."

"I'm not staying in a room that can be locked from the outside."

I finally understood, but I didn't know how to respond. "There's really never been a key, " I began. "The back door key might fit, I suppose. It's a latch key."

I walked to the back door and took out the key. She watched as I tried it in the bedroom lock. It didn't really fit, but by jiggling it around, you could manage to get the lock to engage.

I tried it from inside the room to make sure it could be locked and unlocked and then handed it to her.

"You can use this to lock it from the inside. But we'll need it to get out of the back door in the morning."

"Thank you, Tom," she murmured.

"It's got an aitch."

"What's that?"

"Not 'Tom', 'T-O-M' but 'Thom' with an aitch: 'T-H-O-M'."

"Okay. Thanks, Thom," she deliberately pronounced the 'th' the same way in 'Thom' as she did in 'Thanks'.

"It's a small affectation of mine. I just wanted you to know. I'd prefer it if you still pronounced it 'Tom'".

"Sure."

I left her alone to think about her next move while I headed to the kitchen to make the ham and tomato sandwiches. "Jamón y tomate," I practiced silently. I reflected on the likelihood that the Spanish asperity would be taken for rude in Anglo-centric societies. I had told her my name, but she had made no disclosure of her own. It didn't matter: I had seen Sabasa Garcia many times before.

Some background becomes foreground

> Unexpected visitor became unexpected house guest.

Sabasa elected to remain in my house 'just for one night' and after we had shared a sparse meal of ham and tomato sandwiches on stale bread, she was grateful when I pulled out a fresh towel and new toothbrush for her and told her she could make ready for the night and I'd wake her in the morning. I explained I had a very regular morning routine and she could expect breakfast at eight. While she used the bathroom, I went into Norma's room and extracted the least repulsive of her nighties and folded it on the bed so Sabasa would know she could use it if she wanted to. Then I returned to the living room, opened my computer, and opened my biography of Norma.

Over the years, I have been trying to piece together details of the life of Norma Selfe so that I can leave the world a portrait, however sketchy, of that neglected woman. It is the male role to chronicle life, and if, in modern times, we have chosen to leave that task more and more often to women, it is the future's loss. Men chronicle to preserve; women to explain—and that's self-evidently pointless. I was a little ashamed that I had neglected Norma and her biography over the past months, and because I knew I would have to explain her to Sabasa at some stage, I wanted to refresh my memory and perhaps re-commit myself to her biography.

I read through the few pages of notes I had and made the decision to expand the outline sections of her life as fully as I could over the coming weeks.

Sabasa re-entered the living room, looking very tired, and wished me good night. Then she added, "You never asked me my name."

"Sabasa," I replied.

"What?"

"Sabasa. Your name is 'Sabasa'".

"No it isn't."

"Here it is. You want to escape a dangerous man? Well, leave no traces behind. In this house, your name is Sabasa. It's a pretty name. Spanish. I'm sure I'd prefer it to your own, anyway."

She smiled weakly. "Okay. Whatever. I'll see you in the morning, Thom-with-an-aitch."

*

> *Distraction is the inspiration of the dull. Able to continue work on the Programme and completed the best part of Step 2. Gathered notes for biography.*

The attempt to create an aphorism is indicative of my elevated mood following Sabasa's arrival. I typed a few lines of Norma's biography, jotting down notes of her love of French at school and describing the little handkerchief sampler she had embroidered for her mother. No, I decided, I couldn't go back another generation; so she made the handkerchief for her best friend, Gemma. Bella? Bella. Her best friend, Bella.

Then I went to bed.

*

> *Awoke with a clear head. No erection. Connection? Actually opened my eyes awake; didn't struggle against consciousness and try to sleep; didn't fight it at all. Just awoke.*

I woke next morning at seven. No erection. As my journal notes, I woke surprisingly clear-headed. This was unusual enough for me to write down. I remember wondering if this was a new development or whether on subsequent mornings I would return to my sleep-addled, dissociative fugue-state on waking and need twenty minutes of sunlight and birdsong to convince me to get out of bed. I rose and showered to leave the

Some background becomes foreground

bathroom free for Sabasa when she woke. I made a double portion of porridge and put it on the stove to bubble away. At half past seven, I tapped on Norma's door, "Sabasa? It's seven thirty. The bathroom's free and breakfast will soon be ready. Tea or coffee?"

"Coffee," came a muffled reply. I turned to go—the Spanish and their coffee!—when I heard her joggling the key in the lock and unlocking the door. Norma's bedroom door opened and Sabasa stepped out. She wasn't wearing Norma cotton nightie but had redressed in her clothes of yesterday: a t-shirt and jeans, but her feet were bare. She was breathtakingly beautiful. Her thick, black hair fell in gentle waves about her face. Her skin was creamy white. Her eyes were dark, almost black in that light. I stared. I know I did. She might have walked off the set of a Bond movie. She was heart-achingly beautiful. Her breasts were outlined in the t-shirt but I couldn't look. I stared at her neck, which turned out to be beautiful and sang to be kissed, to be nuzzled, my nose against her neck, warmed by her hair as I kissed her and smelt her scent.

"Good morning, Thom," she said simply and walked past me to the bathroom. "And thanks for letting me sleep here last night. You were right. It was best."

"No problem. Breakfast in ten."

She closed the bathroom door. I heard her slide the tiny bolt to lock it. It was only good to prevent the embarrassment of an accidental opening of the door, but Sabasa wasn't taking chances.

I stood watching a closed bathroom door. I was drugged with her beauty. After a moment's stupor, I headed back to the kitchen to check on breakfast. It didn't feel much like a James Bond moment any more.

Breakfast was less successful than my planning of it had suggested. She didn't like porridge; wasn't interested in scrambled eggs with ham (I only had two eggs and I wanted to sacrifice them for her); ate dry toast and drank coffee.

The conversation was only slightly better.

"I've been thinking a lot about your predicament."

"That's sweet, Thom, but one," she counted off my inadequacies on her fingers to make sure I got the point," you don't know my 'predicament'; two, I have been thinking about it constantly for over a year and I doubt you have any fresh insights to offer; three, I am suspicious of all men equally, except for those who are trying to rescue me, and *those* men I don't trust at all."

"But Four," I made a point of counting it on my hand," I have only ever offered to help you and so far, I have proven to be useful to you." I may have sounded hurt.

"True," she admitted grudgingly. "Look, Thom, I know I sound like a horrible bitch. You're probably a sweet guy who only wants to help, but believe me, after what I've been through, I not only have to rely on myself to get out of it, it's part of the healing that I do this myself."

"Apology accepted," I replied blithely. She turned a savage look on me.

"I never apologised to you, Thom. I'm never apologising to anyone again."

"Understood. Or partially understood, at least. More dry toast?"

"No thanks." She knew she was behaving badly and was unhappy about it, but she clearly couldn't help it.

"His car's gone. I've checked. There are only the usual neighbours' cars outside."

"Thank you. I should get going." Her voice betrayed her uncertainty. Strike, male brain! Strike!

"Without in any way suggesting that I understand your predicament, may I make a suggestion, Sabasa?"

"Sure. I'm not really such a bitch, you know. Good coffee, by the way."

"Thanks. Tasmania."

"The coffee? Tasmanian?"

"No, the coffee's a perfectly drinkable Kenyan/Colombian mix. Tasmania should be your destination for a couple of weeks."

"Tasmania? I don't know anyone in Tasmania!"

"Aha…" I let the exclamation mooch around for a moment. "Precisely."

"Why would I want to go to Tasmania, Thom? It's just putting off the moment of real escape."

"I don't know your situation, but I'm guessing that it isn't trivial. You have escaped from this controlling lunatic, but escape isn't a matter of reaching the tree in the corner of the park and yelling 'Barley!', is it? If it were simple—even as simple as getting a restraining order—you wouldn't have hidden here last night. You are going to have to plan and you are going to have to work at your escape."

"I don't have any money, Thom. I have to go to my sister."

"He knows you don't have money. He knows you have a sister in Sydney. Is he going to begin his search for you in Hobart? No."

"Very convincing, Thom, but I don't have any money. I have nothing. Nothing. These clothes and nothing else. No card, no licence, nothing."

"I warned you I'd been thinking about this, didn't I? Here's the start of a plan—a plan which *you* are going to make and change as you see fit, okay? *Your* plan."

Sabasa looked at me, scrutinised my face. Her rational brain was wrestling with her fear. She knew, rationally, that I was likely to be harmless. She knew that I was probably motivated by the hope of Spanish peach therapy, but she also knew I was not going to batter her to enjoy it. Her fear, her recent experiences, induced a powerful reaction to any male advances. She knew male kindness for what it was.

"Spill," she instructed neutrally.

"While I clear up the breakfast things, you will make a list of the things you need me to buy: clothes, luggage, make-up, pharmaceuticals; everything you need for a seven day absence. I will buy them for you at some dreadful shopping mall thing. I won't guarantee you'll love what I buy, but it will be functional. I will keep all the receipts."

"No." She started shaking her head in disagreement. I ploughed on.

"I will keep all the receipts so you will know exactly how much you owe me. You have to have something to start with or you are finished before you begin. You can try a women's refuge, if you'd prefer, but I think you can be very sure he'll be staking them out."

"I can't take your money."

Technically, it was Norma's money, but I let that pass.

"Indeed you can't. That's why we are taking such care to keep receipts. You are going to repay me. That's got to be part of the healing, too. I am not rescuing you. I am trying to help you as I would want to be helped if I needed it."

"But how do I get to Tasmania, and what the hell do you think I'll do there?"

"Keep an open mind on this…" and I proceeded to explain my plan, which had to involve my friend Shushan, who requires a lot of explanation all on his own.

Briefly, this was the plan I outlined to Sabasa. I would fund her flights to and from Tasmania. She would stay at the Lotus Enlightenment Centre and Hostel, a day spa and meditation retreat twenty-five minutes outside Hobart, operated by my friend Shushan. I have a standing invitation to stay at the Centre for as long as I want to, an invitation I have always taken great care to leave standing, not having any interest in enlightening myself under Shushan's tutelage. However, the Centre had the key qualities we were looking for: it wouldn't cost anything, and it was the safest place to hide in Australia. No one in their right minds stayed there. Sabasa was initially reluctant, but when I explained what a week in the Centre entailed—the simple, vegetarian fare; communal, silent dining; structured meditation classes; the absolute requirement for sexual abstinence; the small group care sessions—she saw the point. It would allow her a whole week to recuperate in safety. She would be free to think, to plan, to start reorganising and re-energising her life. I didn't bother telling her that Shushan was a lunatic. I called him a Buddhist.

"Is Shushan his real name?"

"As real as any other. I knew him first as Kevin, but that was a long time ago. Now, he's Shushan."

"And he's a Buddhist monk?"

"He's a Buddhist. He's more of a seer or a mystic than a monk. An ascetic. He believes in denial of self, which in his case means denying Kevin Ayers."

"Okay," she replied in a small voice. She had no other ideas. I felt a surge of tenderness for her, and although I still had no real idea of the misery she had gone through, I wanted to help and protect her. Had I been wearing a penis collar, it would have been rent asunder.

I cleaned up the breakfast things and Sabasa drew up a list. Hopelessly inadequate, as expected. I sat down with her and we went through the list again, expanding it as necessary. She was reluctant ever to add anything to the list, but I insisted she be prepared. March in Tasmania can mean raging bushfires or the first snows of the year.

Shopping for Sabasa's trip was fun. I found myself enjoying the purchases, following the instructions for bras and panties, stockings, socks, trackie daks, gym shoes, floppy pullovers. I bought a small cosmetic kit recommended by a young woman and a couple of lightweight novels—I knew what the reading materials at the Lotus Enlightenment Centre would be like.

Some background becomes foreground

When I returned to the house, Sabasa was happy with her booty. She insisted on taking control of the receipts, and then turned her attention to getting the clothes washed. I explained the workings of the Lightburn Semi Automatic washing machine—a marvel of mid-century Australian engineering[1]—and faced down the quixotic expression of disbelief when I told her she had to lift the washed clothes into the separate spin dryer.

"Don't knock it until you see how well the spinner works."

"All right, Thom. I just want to get things washed."

As she bustled around, I casually introduced a topic we'd never discussed.

"What was his name?"

She turned her dark eyes on me, flashes of anger in her cheeks.

"Why do you want to know?"

"While you're in Tassie, I need to do a little investigation. I need some information. When you return, I will tell you what I know and you can make your plans."

"What investigation? You have nothing to do with this. You leave this alone. He is dangerous, Thom. This is not some Boy Scout adventure. Genuinely dangerous. You're not the geeky one in the Famous Five."

Apparently I was alone in picturing myself as a raffish, man of the world.

"Right. So I need to know who he is, what he looks like, what car he drives... You'll be in Tasmania, but he'll be looking for you. If he doesn't find you in Sydney, he'll be looking around Melbourne. He's certain to come snooping around here at some time. If I'm to tell you if it's safe or not, I need some

---

[1] Norma had the wonderful 203 model with the continuous tumble washer and separate spin dryer. Unquestionably, the 200 series models were the best washing machines ever produced anywhere.

information. So do you. Unless you plan to live in Kev's ashram permanently, I need to know a little more."

"We'll talk later," was all she said as she headed to the laundry. "I need to think first."

I sulked a little. Quite a lot, I suppose, but then I thought I'd be better off playing it cool. The male brain has three main strategies: ignore it, get angry, play it cool. I dialled my brain to 3 and sat down at my desk in Norma's sewing room. My desk is actually Norma's 1950's Singer Sewing Table (the No. 65 Cabinet) which looks like a small writing desk, but has two hinged flaps which can be opened to make a perfect sewing space for Norma's 1950s Singer Sewing Machine (Model 201). I like working at the cabinet. I feel closer to Norma. The drawers still have their shiny crowds of bobbins and spare needles, coloured threads, and scattering of patterns. Opening the top drawer still generates a tiny cloud of sewing machine oil, a gentle puff of early twentieth century optimism which lubricates the air and makes me smile. I opened my laptop and resumed work on Norma's life.

*

The Early Years

Extract from "Bridge of Generations, the unauthorised biography of Norma Selfe", unpublished

In the afternoon of 9th of May, 1931, unaware that Doug Strang and Jack Titus had kicked 14 goals between them as Richmond trounced North Melbourne, kicking a then record score of 30.19 (199) to North's 4.7 (31), Norma Selfe was born in her parents' house in Rowena Parade, Richmond, her first, feeble cries mingling with the delighted roar of the Punt Road Oval crowd. Norma was to remain a loyal, if passive, Richmond supporter for the rest of her life, the thin yellow and black scarf she knitted for herself as a child wrapped around the neck of her teddy bear, a treasured memento of childhood which was buried with her in 2015.

Although life in Richmond in the thirties is often portrayed as rough and dangerous—a working class suburb in the middle of the Great Depression; home of criminal gangs, illegal betting shops, and brothels; a place where opium and heroin use were commonplace—it was not remembered that way by Norma. Norma's family lived in a well-maintained house on Richmond Hill, which, in those days meant there was a clear distinction between her family and the working class families living the tiny, wooden houses in the old malarial swamps, long since drained, but still remembered. She was happy growing up in Richmond. She enjoyed being sent to the shops for groceries, buying sausages and chops from the butcher on Bridge Road, being given bouquets of flowers ('Still perfectly good!') by the lady who played the organ at Kings Funerals. If there was danger in Richmond, it was danger for the outsiders, for the rowdies who came from Collingwood to watch the football and brawl in the bars which lined Punt Road; there was no danger for a respectable young lass who knew the suburb and was known. Richmond looked after its own.

Norma went to school at the Vaucluse Convent on Richmond Hill. Although her family was staunchly Congregationalist, they were practical in financial matters. The Convent provided a good education at a reasonable cost, and it was only twenty or thirty yards from their door. Even a Catholic education was better than having to attend the State School; so Norma completed her primary school education with the Catholics, leaving her father to worry about the cost of the uniform and books, and her mother to worry about her religious instruction.

© Copyright 2016, Thom Furphy

*

Sabasa looked around the corner.

"Are you working now?"

I smiled at her to let her know I wasn't sulking.

"Yes, but don't worry; it's nothing that can't be interrupted." I pointed her to the sewing stool which stood in the corner. It was embroidered with Norma's cross-stitch interpretation of hakea flowers and leaves. She sat down carefully on the stool, as if worried it wouldn't support her weight. She needn't have worried; she would have weighed not much more than Norma in her prime.

"What is it that you do?" she asked.

"For work, you mean?"

"Yes. Are you a teacher or something? You don't seem to need to go out to work much."

"No, I'm a writer. A political commentator mostly, but I also write biographies and scientific works for the popular market."

I could see she was quite impressed. My house is not luxurious, but it is comfortably furnished and it's in a good suburb.

"I didn't think you could make money writing."

"Most can't, of course," I agreed. I certainly couldn't, but I didn't think she needed to know that at this awkward time. It might have made her reluctant to borrow money from me. "That's why I always have a few irons in the fire. I use my blog to help drive sales of other projects." For some reason, people seem to think a blog can make money.

"I've been thinking about what you said. I would like to tell you about myself, about what happened to me. I think I need to tell someone."

"I think it's important, too."

"I just can't tell you yet. I need some time."

"That's all right," I said gently, but disappointed, "when you're ready, I'm here."

"I'd like to stay a few days..."

"Of course. We'll need a few days anyway."

"What for?" she asked, again suspicious.

"You said you had no licence, no credit card."

"No, I've got nothing."

"We're going to need some form of identification. You can't fly anywhere these days without some form of ID."

She looked crestfallen. I had a strong urge to get out of my chair and hold her. She looked up and said in a steely voice, "I'll kill him."

The urge to hug dissipated.

"Hmmm. Let's pop that idea in the Possible But Unhelpful basket and think again, shall we?"

"He has all my documents. Everything."

Quick Quiz: What would the Male Brain respond to this situation?

- A. Time you went to the police, my dear. They are experts in dealing with this sort of thing.
- B. Never mind. Shall we start the process of having your documents re-issued?
- C. I think I can help with that...

If you answered A or B, you are a woman.

"I think I can help with that," I offered.

"How?"

"You know the layout of the property. You know where he's likely to keep your documents. I know how to gain access without being detected. So, some time when we know he's absent, let's go and get your possessions."

I watched her. Emotions flashed across her face like sunlight on rippled water. She was scared and angry and strangely cool. I could see her making complex calculations, equations in a calculus I couldn't understand.

"You know how to break into a house?"

"Second nature to me." This was an exaggeration. If I broke into his house, it would be the second house I'd broken into. Still, you couldn't say I had *no* experience as a house-breaker.

She gave me a quizzical look. She didn't believe me, but she wanted to.

"He has it alarmed."

"He has me alarmed as well, but we can manage that if we're quick. Alarms are only useful to cause panic."

"I know the code. Unless he's changed it..."

Some background becomes foreground

"We're laughing then. He hasn't changed it. He knows you're too scared to come back."

"Okay, Thom," she smiled, "let's pretend you know how to break into a house and I'm prepared to risk setting foot inside that place again. How do we guarantee he won't be there?"

I hadn't thought that far ahead, but trusty friend, male brain, was ready with the answer.

"Bait." I paused dramatically, but she only waited. "He's looking for you. So let's give you to him."

"Are you insane?"

"Wait. Let's say you ask to meet him in a very public place. Tell him you want to meet him in a neutral space to organise a civilized separation. Tell him you're not interested in blame; you just want to be able to move on with your life."

"You really think I'm going to meet him?"

"No. You're going to *arrange* to meet him. Somewhere he won't expect. Somewhere we know will take him at least forty minutes to return from when you don't show up."

"You've got somewhere in mind?"?

"Where's his place? This side of town?"

She nodded grimly. Even remembering the address was painful for her.

"Well, I don't know your man, but I'm guessing he's not familiar with the National Gallery. Tell him you'll meet him inside, near the front, near the water wall. That way, he's got to drive through town, park, get to the gallery, hang around worrying if he's in the right spot, wait ten, fifteen, perhaps twenty minutes until he's sure you're not coming, and then, even if he drives straight back to his place, we're long gone."

She continued nodding, her eyes fixed on the floor, her mouth set in a tight line. I shouldn't have thought her beautiful, but she was breathtakingly, gut-wrenchingly, heartachingly beautiful.

I spoke to her gently. "You have to reassert your identity. You have to reclaim your self from this man."

She turned and looked at me in the eyes.

"He's really dangerous, Thom. I'm not joking. If he finds us, he'll kill us."

"He won't find us. He won't kill us. His name is Rumpelstiltskin and we know it."

Sabasa threw her arms around my neck and squeezed me tight.

"Thank you, Thom," she murmured into my neck. My neck waited in case there was to be any further murmuring. There wasn't. Sabasa unwound herself from around me like a small tissue collar falling off a penis and stood and walked towards the laundry.

"I'll see about the washing," she whispered quietly. Then she turned and added, "Bluebeard. Not Rumpelstiltskin. Bluebeard."

I sat where I was, detumescing slowly. To speed the process, I decided to turn my thoughts to political reform. It helped. It always does.

*

Why do we elect representatives?

Extract from A Programme of Moderate Political Reform in Australia, www.pmpra.com

There is a basic element of modern democracies that is almost never questioned: why do we elect people to represent us? At first sight, the answer seems obvious. We can't all go and sit in parliament, nor would we want to; so we elect people to represent us to do that job for us. But is it really as simple as that? Why, for example, are we forced to have someone represent us? If I chose to attend parliament, why shouldn't I? Admittedly, my vote in parliament shouldn't carry the same weight as someone who represented thousands of others, but why can't I represent myself? Why can't I choose to be represented for some decisions, but cast my vote personally on issues about which I feel strongly?

Some background becomes foreground

Historically, representation of thousands of voters by a single, literate, educated person made sense. When a large proportion of the population couldn't read, it made sense that someone capable of reading legislation should be elected to look after their interests, but we have had a highly literate population for a long time now.

When the only way to conduct government was to convene to a central location because physical presence was required to vote, to discuss, to canvass, representation by a single person made perfect sense; but this is no longer the case. A common physical location is no longer a requirement for discussion, information dissemination, or decision making. Parliament can be as big as we choose.

It might be argued that the point of electing representatives was to ensure that the will of the people was represented by electing someone who shared the opinions of the voters of the electorate. But isn't there a simpler and much more accurate way of ensuring that the opinions of the people are heard? A statistically relevant random selection of citizens is far more likely to lead to expressions of the popular will than any complicated chicanery involving political parties and systems of voting. Every four years, we should select, at random, citizens to fulfil political service.

Before you dismiss the idea out of hand, consider that we already use this system to make decisions which are of far more importance than most of the decisions taken in parliament. We readily accept that a jury of a mere twelve citizens, selected at random and with no special training, should make decisions which immediately affect the lives, livelihoods, and safety of their fellow citizens. What is more, almost all legal experts continue to insist that trial by jury is the best and safest method of ensuring there is justice in our land. Why should politics be any different? We trust juries to make decisions which range from complex financial cases, through involved forensic tangles, to murder and treason. There are simply no more important decisions made than those we trust to juries. Our political system deserves the same high standard of impartial diligence.

I will discuss a proposed mechanism for selection, preparation, and administration of a polity comprising randomly selected citizens in a later post. I will also elaborate a mechanism to allow citizens who are not selected for parliamentary duty to participate in all parliamentary voting without compromising the rights of citizens who prefer a representative as a proxy. For this step, it is enough to state that our parliament should be populated with citizens selected in the same way as jury panels are. All citizens should be prepared to serve in parliament for four years as a civic responsibility.

© Copyright 2016, Thom Furphy

The plot to beard Bluebeard

> *Great wits are sure to madness near allied,*
> *and thin partitions do their bounds divide.*
> *Dryden, I think. There is a type of madness to which*
> *even little wits succumb. I cannot write its name. The*
> *madness which cannot be named. Breakfast is killing*
> *me. I wake without erections, but I spend the day*
> *tormented by them. Visit to Dr N expensive.*

Re-reading my journal entry, I realize how far I had regressed. Sabasa had made me an adolescent again. I was developing a crush on her. Poetry! Question: Dryden? Dryden? How out of practice was I? But out of practice or not, I was experiencing love in a way I never dreamt I was capable of. It gave me new insight into Norma's first love which I hastily documented the next morning while the coffee brewed and before Sabasa woke.

*

First Love

Extract from "Bridge of Generations, the unauthorised biography of Norma Selfe", unpublished

At seventeen, Norma was an attractive, but inexperienced, unfulfilled woman. She lived with her parents in her childhood home in Richmond, but the neighbourhood she grew up in, in which she felt so familiar and so much a part of, was changing. New families were moving in. The first of the wave of 'Mediterranean migrants' which would colour Melbourne's character for the next half century began to arrive; servicemen returning from war, demobbed from the military or released from prisoner of war camps created an uneasy disruption to civilian life; the old inhabitants were moving on, retiring, dying. For Norma, the world of Richmond was small, but exciting, changing, and filled with new possibilities. She, herself, was one of the agents of the change she felt. Now, when she walked to the milk bar to get the milk, eggs, and papers in the morning, she felt male eyes upon her. She became aware of the new attention she drew from men.

The plot to beard Bluebeard

One of those men was a dark-eyed Italian who had been released from the Bonegilla migrant camp earlier that year. Giuseppe Garcia had been a medical student in pre-war Milan, but in Richmond in 1949, he was renting a single, small room in Grattan Place and working as a house painter for a local firm. 'Joe' was dark, slim, handsome, and courteous. Unlike the Australian men who only seemed able to leer or shout stupidities to attract her attention, Joe would smile shyly, even bow slightly from the waist. Norma fell in love.

Their first meetings were nothing more than shy collisions in the street, outside the milk bar, walking to the tram stop. Even dressed in his paint spattered work clothes, Joe looked dashing, courtly, elegant. Norma found herself looking for him in the street. She began to make her visits to the shops regular, hoping she would see him, hoping he would remember her schedule of visits. Her mother was exasperated at how often she forgot the simplest things and needed to retrace her steps to the shops. And her moods! She could burst into tears and shut herself in her room for no reason!

Joe was aware of the effect he had on Norma. He could imagine her quick, bird-like heart fluttering in panic and excitement beneath her blouse. He watched with amused anticipation as the girl made subtle changes to her look, her hair, her clothes, just for a dash to the shops. He knew the signs and he approved. She was a beautiful, young woman and Joe was ready to find a beautiful, young wife. He knew that Italian men did not easily find favour as husbands in Australian households. The women had no difficulty in accepting a European accent into the house, but Australian fathers viewed things differently. Joe knew he needed patience to win this prize.

One day, as Norma was walking past him, he called out to her, "Senorita, may I ask a favour?"

She turned, blushing and smiling. "How can I help?"

"I am writing to my mother in Italy and I wonder if you can help me with one or two English words?"

Joe spoke a clear, delightfully accented English. Norma was almost giddy with listening to him.

"Of course. What words?"

Joe drew a few sheets of paper from his pocket: a long, hand-written letter to his mother in Italian.

"You see here, Senorita, I have written..." he paused, as if thinking about the translation, "I have met a beautiful, young Australian woman whom I should like to ask out. You would like her, mother. She is young and graceful and dresses as beautifully as the women in Rome. Her name is..."

He stopped and looked at Norma, smiling, his brown eyes luminous with laughter and longing.

Norma looked at him, blushing. "Who do you mean?" she asked.

"You, Senorita. What is your name?"

"Norma."

Joe bowed gently from the waist.

"I am so delighted to meet you, Norma. Now I shall finish the letter to my mother. I hope I can tell her that we are going to the dance at the Town Hall on Saturday?"

Norma, who had never been to a dance, agreed at once.

© Copyright 2016, Thom Furphy

*

I, myself, was a combination of Norma and Joe. I was infatuated with Sabasa. I was alight with the first stirrings of love. My body tingled with an energy and a warmth that I had never felt before. We breakfasted a little more successfully than the previous morning. I had bought some orange juice and fresh bread rolls, some unsalted butter, some over-priced Iberian jamon, and some fresh coffee beans. Sabasa wore nothing more than a t-shirt and knickers and I fussed about with breakfast while my penis made light of its quondam psychosomatic condition.

After breakfast, Sabasa sent me out with a shopping list for groceries and then spent the day washing and drying the rest of the clothes I had bought her. After convincing her that the back of the house was safe and couldn't be seen from the road, she even ventured out into the backyard to hang washing on Norma's Hills hoist. She surprised me by asking me to buy a couple more items for her that we'd forgotten, including luggage for her flight – Norma's large, sturdy suitcase having been rejected as too heavy and too ugly.

I was happy to buy things for her. Every request was a sacred condition of the quest I had accepted. I knew I was ridiculous, but I didn't care. I would have done anything for her.

While I was out battling the crowds and the aesthetic assault of a shopping mall, Sabasa made lunch for us and spread a rug out on the grass in the backyard so we could have a picnic. She had spread the rug next to Norma's ornamental pond, which was fully stocked with pondweed, water plants, algae, and overfed goldfish. The fish were overfed because of the plague of wrigglers in the pond.

"The mozzies will tear us apart," I pointed out, when I returned with my trophies and she explained her plan.

She looked at me with her chocolate brown eyes, "But it's fine today. And I need to be outside, Thom. I *need* it." She emphasised the word in a voice that revealed a pain that had its birth many, many months before, the memory of which was crouched and ready to sink its claws into her mind at any moment.

"Mozzies never trouble me much," I conceded. "And I love nothing more than eating outside in the fresh air!" This was not so much a concession as a bald-faced lie, but she smiled with delight, took me by the hand and led me to the blanket where she sat me down and started doling out sandwiches and coffee. She looked like a girl playing tea parties. I was aching with love for her.

We munched our way through the picnic. The mosquitoes made do with a couple of pints of my blood and my bum went to sleep, but I didn't care. I wanted to talk about the plan to break into her former house, but I didn't want to spoil our lunch. Instead, I burbled about the shopping centre, about choosing the luggage, about hunting for the cosmetics she asked for. She laughed and teased and was happy.

First Love continued

Extract from "Bridge of Generations, the unauthorised biography of Norma Selfe", unpublished

Their accidental meetings increased in frequency until they had become first, unexceptional, and then frankly planned. Sometimes they would walk to the park across Punt Road, walking beneath the elms and oaks, stopping at favourite benches to sit, pretend an interest in the pigeons or other people strolling through the park, but mainly to talk, to hold hands shyly and secretly.

One day, after discussing Joe's life in Italy, Norma asked him about Italian food and spaghetti, the only Italian dish she had heard of and one she had never tried. Joe painted elaborate and mouth-watering pictures of Italian food. He derided the brittle, dry stalks of flour which passed for spaghetti in Australia and offered to show Norma how real Italian pasta was made, how a real Italian sauce was made, and how a real Italian and his girlfriend could eat it. The date was made. Next Thursday, Joe would take the afternoon off work on the pretext of needing to renew his work permit. His boss wouldn't mind, he insisted, because work was slow at the moment and it meant a saving of half a day's wages. Thursday was the landlady's day to help at the church shop. Joe would have free run of the kitchen and as long as he cleaned up by four, no one need ever know.

"It will be like a little trip to Italy for you. A taste of the real trip we will make one day."

Norma called on all her powers of propriety, but Joe held both her hands, looked into her eyes, and begged her, smiling, not to break his heart. Propriety shattered into a thousand glistening pieces.

On Thursday, Norma, not yet quite eighteen, put on a simple, dark dress, flecked with small red roses. She brushed and arranged her hair to mimic Barbara Stanwyck and set off on a four hour trip to Italy.

Joe met her at the door of the guest house. He was looking slightly flustered, his hands and trousers dusted with flour.

"You look like you've been busy!" she laughed.

Joe ushered her inside, then inspected her with hungry admiration.

"You look so beautiful. I have never seen you in that dress."

He drew her to him and kissed her, gently, but passionately, deeply. They had never had the freedom to be so openly in love.

"Joe!" She breathed. She didn't tell him to stop because she didn't want him to.

"The pasta is drying. Look." He hurried her into the dark kitchen and showed her long lengths of pasta, wheat yellow, draped over the backs of chairs.

"We can cut the spaghetti when the sheets are dry."

Joe drew her body against his again and kissed her. She surrendered to his kisses, almost fainting with her delight and passion and surprise. He led her, unresisting to his room. Suddenly fearful, she looked at the bed and whispered, "No. No, Joe."

Joe moved slowly towards her and kissed her again. She felt his arms envelope her, his broad, strong hands pressing the length of her spine against him. He reached behind her neck and undid the single, small button which closed her dress. Then he reached down and gathered the hem and began to lift it over her.

"Joe," she whispered. It was neither encouragement nor opposition. She was in his hands. She was his. Her body was revealed before him. She had covered her small breasts with one arm. He drew it gently to one side, bent his head to her chest, and began kissing her nipples. New delight flooded her. New delight and new terror. He led her to the bed and sat her on it. He knelt before her and removed her shoes and stockings. He kissed her feet, her ankles, her calves. He ran his hands along her legs and whispered to her in Italian, words she didn't understand as words but as feelings, as breath inside her. He stood before her, undid his belt and let it hang open. He leant forward and pushed her shoulders tenderly onto the bed. She closed her eyes and felt his hands travel down her body, touch her breasts and stomach, then grasp the elastic of her cami-knickers and begin to ease them off. She shut her eyes and felt her body flooding with love for this strong, gentle, worthy man as she heard him undressing quickly, and then she felt the heat of a lithe male body next to her on the bed.

"Norma," he whispered. "Open your eyes."

She obeyed and turned her head to look into his eyes.

The plot to beard Bluebeard

"Your eyes are so beautiful, Norma."

His hands began playing over her body, his words changed into Italian, soft as birdsong. He reached his hand between her legs as he kissed her, his tongue brushing her lips, and then, as she waited for something she knew must happen, he pushed one broad, strong finger inside her, deeper and deeper. She gasped. The Italian words flowed like honey over her body, his fingers exploring her deeper, gently, deeper.

He moved his body above her. She looked into his eyes. She was terrified and delighted. Her legs moved to accommodate his body. He reached down and positioned his cock between her open lips and pushed himself inside her. It seemed to Norma that his cock went on and on inside her. Deeper than she knew possible. He kissed her, but she was incapable of kissing. She was gasping for breath, delighted with the warmth and weight of his body. He withdrew and then pushed inside her again. It felt deeper. She heard herself moan a small, breathy gasp of voiced relief, and Joe began to fuck her, tenderly, firmly.

© Copyright 2016, Thom Furphy

*

Nothing like that happened on our picnic rug, but after our picnic, I raced to document Norma's first encounter with Joe while Sabasa—at her own insistence—tidied up outside and washed the dishes.

In the afternoon, Sabasa looked in on me working in the sewing room.

"We need to talk about our plans."

Our plans. *Our* plans. My heart raced to hear it.

"But first," she continued softly, "I want to thank you for everything. For putting up with me. For freezing to death on the grass before. For letting me take my time."

I shrugged and started to say something dismissive.

"No. I appreciate it, Thom. Thank you."

I was strangely embarrassed. I felt shy and awkward—particularly as the last words I had typed were "began to fuck her, tenderly, firmly". I was turned uncomfortably in my chair, hoping my body was adequately hiding the laptop screen. I turned and shut the laptop screen quickly.

"All right. Plans. Let's talk."

Sabasa stepped into the room and perched herself on the embroidered stool.

"What are you thinking?" She asked eagerly.

The male brain was still reverberating to 'tenderly, firmly' and had to wheel its attention around to the quasi-suicidal plan to break into the house of a violent psychopath and retrieve some of Sabasa's property.

"A few questions first," I blustered. "Talk me through the layout of the house. Anything I should know? Alarms, dogs, booby traps, bodies?"

"It's a two bedroom suburban house. New. Newish. Narrow because it is one of a pair built on a single block. Enter through the front door to a corridor. The two bedrooms are off to the right, one after the other. The front bedroom is set up as a gym. The second bedroom is the master bedroom..."

She paused a moment before she could continue.

"... was our bedroom. It has a lock on the door. There is an ensuite. Next down the corridor is the bathroom and laundry, then the living room which opens onto the kitchen and an open dining space. From the kitchen, the back door leads directly to the backyard which is tiny. A garage at the end of the yard has a door to the garden and opens onto the laneway at the back. He keeps the car parked at the front. Never in the garage. The garage is a discipline area."

She was staring at the floor. Her voice had become gradually softer and less distinct. I waited a moment, thinking about what I should say. Before I could decide, she raised her face and looked me in the eye.

"I will kill that bastard if I see him again," she said in a calm, steely voice.

"Nothing special about the locks or alarms?"

"No. He didn't need it. Sometimes he would leave me and leave the front door unlocked. I knew what he wanted. He wanted me to try to escape. I knew he was waiting."

I didn't say anything. I couldn't say anything. I did the only thing I could think of: I kept returning to the plan. Our plan.

"Back door? Is it wood, glass? Is there a security door?"

"There's a security door at the front, but only a screen door at the back. It's just a wooden frame door, I think. Nothing special."

"Windows at the back?"

"There's a glass panel next to the back door. Too narrow to fit through, but you could smash it to let yourself in the back door if the keys are in it."

"Can we get around to the back door if we enter from the street?"

"Not easily. The whole place is fenced at the back at a height to keep anyone from looking in. The side gate is locked. You'd have to climb over it."

"Do you know what he's got hooked up to the alarm?"

"The alarm has sensors on the front door and the windows in the front room—his gym. Apart from that, there are motion sensors in the house: one in the corridor; one in the living room; one near the back door."

"And what does the alarm do? Does he pay for a security service to come out?"

"No. He's too cheap for that. He installed it all himself. It's a DIY job. It just makes a sickening noise when it goes off."

"Do you know if he's hooked up any cameras?"

She paused for a moment, gathering her strength to talk.

"There are several cameras in the garage. He records the discipline sessions. He sometimes videos in the bedroom, but that's only for special occasions. There are no security cameras." She looked up, angry at me for making her feel vulnerable. "So what's the plan?"

"Well, there won't be any problem gaining entry. We should aim to be in and out within ten minutes. We should try for five. We'll enter from the street; jemmy the side gate and walk down the side of the house and enter through the back door. We'll break the glass panel if we can see keys in the back door; otherwise brute force on the back door."

It sounded so plausible. As if I knew what I was talking about and had done it before. As she asked her next question, I was thinking, "Where do you buy a jemmy?"

"What about the alarm?"

"Ear plugs and leaflets."

"What?"

"We wear ear plugs to prevent damaging our hearing. You know, the sort of inadequate thing they sell to kids at rock concerts."

"Yes, I understand 'ear plugs'. It was the next bit. Leaflets?"

"Ah, yes. I was writing the text of those when you came in." 'Tenderly, firmly' was coming easier and easier. I adlibbed the words I might have been writing had I been thinking about our plan, "'Apex Security will be installing and testing a new alarm system in [INSERT PSYCHOPATH'S ADDRESS HERE] at whatever hour we decide to have him enjoying the artworks at the National Gallery. We apologise for any inconvenience, but please ring our office to arrange a quotation and we will offer you an additional 5% off our already low prices!'"

I smiled and continued with the plan. "We will drop leaflets in his neighbour's letterboxes. He doesn't strike me as the type to have much to do with the neighbours if he can help it; so I don't think there's any danger of them racing out to discuss it with him."

"None. He's always deliberately rude to them to make sure they don't get nosey."

"Perfect. They will hear the alarm and do nothing. We will be in and out. Now, you need to make a list of everything you want and can carry. Making the list before you go will mean you won't be flustered trying to decide what to grab and you're less likely to forget something important. Because I don't plan on doing this a second time..."

I neglected to mention that we would leave through the garage out the back. It didn't seem important and I needed to get to my late afternoon appointment with Dr No at Apex Medical. We agreed that Sabasa would make the dinner and have a quiet evening in while I went to my doctor's appointment.

"What's wrong with you?"

"Nothing. It's just a check up."

"I didn't think men had check ups."

"Some of us do."

Sabasa looked at me closely. "Should you be doing what we're planning on doing, Thom?"

"Of course not. But neither should you; so that's okay. No health problems, I promise."

At least, no health problems I wanted to talk to Sabasa about, particularly as I was hoping she might be providing me the cure. I left her promising to make a list of all she wanted and its likely locations and 'something edible for dinner'.

"Don't answer the door," I cautioned, as much to give her the impression that someone might call as to protect her from her lunatic.

*

The same bored woman was on reception at Apex Medical Centre. The same resentful Dr No called me into his consulting room and began his staccato interrogation before the door closed.

"So. Mr Furphy. Erections, yes no?"

"Well, yes *and* no. Yes, the sticky tape test reveals that I'm still having nocturnal erections, but no, nothing visible in the morning."

"Good!" Dr No rubbed his hands together and fixed me with a hard look. "Psychological problems are so much more expensive to treat than medical! I think I need to refer you back to your local GP for a long course of psychotherapy!"

"I don't think so, Dr No. I'm happy to let nature take its course now that I know there's no physical problem. Besides, I seem to be able to get an erection during the day…"

"Ah! You are paying for sex! Is that a good idea? Dr No says, 'No!' Paying for sex is not good."

"No, I'm not paying for sex!"

Dr No turned and pulled out a hypodermic syringe and started removing it from its sterile wrapping.

"Promiscuous women no better for you. Roll up your sleeve please. Blood test."

"What for," I asked as I rolled up my sleeve, unthinkingly compliant.

"Checking for STIs. Complete. Not expensive, but necessary for you."

"But I haven't had any sex lately!"

"Can't be too careful. Small prick."

I may have transcribed that incorrectly. He may have said, "Can't be too careful, small prick." But as he was inserting a needle into my arm, I have to give him the benefit of the doubt.

"Results will be sent to your local GP. Please make sure you make an appointment to collect them."

I left his consulting room and headed for the bored receptionist. Dr No called out behind me, "Full STI check for Mr Furphy! Results to GP. No further appointment necessary!"

The plot to beard Bluebeard

The receptionist made out my bill and pushed a medicare form and a pen towards me. I told her I preferred to come as a private patient. She raised an eloquent eyebrow which conveyed her (as it happens, completely incorrect) understanding of why I wanted no record of this encounter and printed a new bill. After I had paid, I picked up the pen from the desk to hand back to her. She looked at it as if it were a cane toad and snarled curtly, "You keep it," and drew a new pen out of her desk drawer.

Weekend Execution

> No erection. Doctor assures me again I am normal. This should be re-assuring therefore. It isn't. I have sexual feelings. I am normal. Why don't I have morning erections anymore? If this symptom were new, I would be tempted to put it down to love. Which would be unfortunate, but possible. Love is accorded many wonderful qualities. Perhaps it has the power to quench desire while fomenting it. Shakespeare may have made note of this quality. Or was that beer? Why have I found love now? Why is my brain now flooded with oxytocin?

Why indeed, male brain? Except that the most perfunctory research reveals that my brain had first been flooded with testosterone, oestrogen, dopamine, and serotonin, and only later would it be flooded with oxytocin and vasopressin if I managed to convince Sabasa to stay with me.

I have a regrettable habit of getting ahead of myself.

Our mornings already felt like our routine. I would spring out of bed, clear-headed and joyful. I would make breakfast, gradually accommodating our preferences while always trying to convince her of the superiority of tea over coffee, porridge over muesli or toast or nothing, and marmalade over everything. I was making little progress, except in the matter of the marmalade. Norma left me an embarrassment of three fruit marmalade which is sweet, and bitter, and finely textured and just beautiful. Every jar is a celebration of the senses: taste, touch, smell, sight. Placing a small jar on the table where it caught the light and glowed with the exquisite orange lustre of a gem filled me with joy. It may just have been the dopamine, of course.

Sabasa had overcome her darker suspicions of me and was relaxed in my company. She still locked her door at night, but this was her equivalent of a warm cup of cocoa. In the mornings, she would join me, dressed in something so wildly seductive—t-shirt and knickers, or t-shirt and pyjama trousers, or t-shirt and anything—that my sexual function was convincingly apparent to me (while remaining entirely unobtrusive to her, I add). When she entered the kitchen, hair unbrushed, smelling of warmth and bed, honey and butter, gold and jet, the morning was lit. She knew the effect she had on me. No matter how matter-of-factly I tried to wish her 'Good morning', she responded with a smile which drew me into beaming like a loon. Only once she had received her morning's grinning obeisance did she settle herself into one of Norma's emu-back kitchen chairs[2], smooth her hair or spread her fingers and run them up the back of her neck and through her dark, thick hair, and torture me with complaints about breakfast.

"Would you like some eggs this morning?"

"I need to get out, Thom."

"Eggs. I asked about eggs."

"No eggs, thank you," she replied, reaching for a triangle of toast I had put in Norma's poorly silver-plated toast rack. "I need to get out. I know what you think, but I can't afford to feel like a prisoner here."

I must have looked hurt, because she leapt up from her chair and held my hands, looking into my face imploringly and urgently.

---

[2] Emu pattern kitchen chairs were made by the Melbourne Chair Company, 20 Down Street, Collingwood from 1894 to the 1920s. They had round, turned front legs and rectangular one-piece back legs, joined with seven lengths of round dowel. The backs of the chairs were steam-pressed with a design of two emus against a rising sun, framed by flowering eucalyptus sprays and ferns. They were very comfortable and very beautiful, especially when they carried the additional decoration of Sabasa.

"Thom, please try to understand. I need to feel safe here. I *do* feel safe here, but at night, when I'm thinking about things, I start to question myself, start to think I might be letting myself be controlled by another man."

Her eyes scanned my face, looking for evidence of understanding, of fellow feeling.

"You have been wonderful to me, Thom. I'm not saying this to hurt you. I'm saying this to be honest and because I need to feel that this is a safe place for me, you need to help me come and go so I don't feel trapped.

She kept looking into my face. Luckily. Sexual function was no longer as well camouflaged as it ought to have been.

I turned away, fussing about with a saucepan and eggs, covertly checking to see if my erection was noticeable.

"I understand, Sabasa. And you're right. Give me a moment to think about it."

Sabasa returned to the table and sat down again. I continued talking to the eggs while I waited for my penis to revert to its more usual state.

"I agree that we need to make you *feel* safe here, and while I can't ever understand exactly what you went through, I want you to know…" I looked over my shoulder at her while keeping my penis jammed against the cold metal of Norma's cook top, "… that I will always, *always*, trust what you tell me you need. If you need to go out…" I returned to face the eggs, "… I believe you need to go out and I will help you make it happen."

I heard the chair scrape on the floor, and suddenly I was wrapped in Sabasa's arms as she hugged me from behind.

"Thank you, Thom. Thank you so much."

She squeezed me, pushing her body against me. I squeezed myself hard against Norma's stove.

"Careful, careful!" I laughed. "Boiling water here!"

The water was nowhere near boiling, but I was. Sabasa returned to her chair. I continued fussing with the saucepan for a few moments, allowing calmness to descend through my body. When I finally turned to face her again, she was chomping her way through her triangle of toast, sniffling back a tear, but smiling, laughing softly at me.

I sat at the table and felt my spirits sinking. I enjoyed keeping her here. I enjoyed her dependence on me. Everything I did to help her was helping her decide to leave.

"You're looking very serious suddenly."

"Sorry." I returned with a weak smile, "Just thinking things through."

"Well, what's the plan, Poirot?"

All thoughts of despondency fled in the light of her smile.

"The reason I was looking serious," I lied, "was that I was thinking that there's no point in you just 'getting out' of this house. We need to reclaim your possessions and get you to Tasmania. No point in putting it off. Let's get moving on getting into his house and then let's get you out of danger."

Her smile disappeared and she answered softly, "Okay."

"It's not quite quarter to eight. Saturday. Does he work on the weekends?"

"Probably not. It depends on his shifts. He can be rostered on any hours, but usually these days it's nine to five in the week."

Hint: Ask about his job, male brain! Ask about his job!

"Good. His job won't interfere with anything." Nice work, male brain. "All right, we have to initiate the meeting. Let's work on your script."

"My script?"

"Yes. You're going to follow a script and not deviate from it. We're keeping this short and sweet. You are not discussing anything except the meeting."

"What if he doesn't agree to meet?"

"So much the better. You hang up and we wait a couple of days. Next time, he'll agree to meet. But I don't think we'll have to worry about it. He'll want to meet."

I got a pad of paper and one of Norma's souvenir ballpoint pens from the desk. As I returned to the kitchen table, I saw Sabasa's face, pale with anxiety, her mouth tight, the pulse in her neck visible. She turned to look at me as I approached.

"I don't want to call him, Thom."

"I know. You're scared…"

"No. I don't want to call him. I want to kill him," she said coldly, and not for the first time, I noted. Her beautiful, dark, chocolate coloured eyes looked blankly fierce.

"Another excellent idea we'll just note down…" I scratched 'Kill him' on the pad, "… and then we'll think about it a bit…" I made a show of putting my hand to my chin as if in deep thought, "… and then we'll just SCRATCH IT OUT!" I drew several firm lines through the words.

"Killing people creates difficulties, Sab," I said. I didn't tell her I knew about those difficulties. Killing might be straightforward, but disposing of a body is not simple. "And we're going to be working on *removing* difficulties from your life, not creating any more."

Magically, her eyes flooded with life again.

"Okay. Thanks, Thom. Let's talk script."

*

It took us the best part of two hours, but at the end of that time, we had a script. We practiced how we would use it, with me playing the part of an aggressive psychopath. We tried to anticipate various responses, but as soon as it started to get too complicated, we agreed that we would keep it very simple. Just because he asked questions, didn't mean Sabasa had to answer them. At various points, he would almost certainly try to control the conversation. I stressed to her the need to remain detached and in control. Sabasa had an almost hysterical fear[3] of her ex tracing the phone; so we agreed that I would walk to the nearest supermarket and buy a mobile phone and pay-as-you-go phone card. We would conduct the conversation on speaker phone. Sabasa would speak, of course, but she would take direction from me. If her ex asked her a question, I would point to one of the answers on the response sheet and Sabasa would answer with that response. Under no circumstances would she deviate from the message script or the response script. If there was no suitable response, she would either repeat her last statement, remain silent, or hang up. In our script, we marked several points at which she would tell him that if he didn't follow her instructions she would hang up and we agreed that she would let me be the judge of when to disconnect.

Message script:

If his response is Calm	If his response is Aggressive
"At some point, we are going to have to talk about what happened, but before that, I need to get all my possessions out of your house so I can start my life again."	"If you won't agree to discuss this with me calmly, I will hang up." *If he continues in an aggressive manner; hang up here.* **Disconnection Point.**

---

[3] Women readers will not need to read this footnote. For male readers: for 'hysterical', please substitute the phrase 'rational and well-founded'.

Response Accepting
If he sounds agreeable to meeting – the most likely response because he'll feel in control:
"I want to meet somewhere public and I want your agreement that there will be no drama. We are meeting to plan how I can pick up my possessions without you being there, or how you can deliver me those possessions if you don't want me in your house alone.
"Do you agree?"

Response Other
Any other response – suggesting you're taking this too seriously; suggesting he wants you back; he's missed you; he's been so worried; anything else:
"I will only discuss how we can meet to agree how I can recover my possessions. If you insist on talking about anything else, I will hang up." **Disconnection Point.**

You will now set up the meeting time and place. You will make clear that you will accept no other meeting place or time.
"I want to meet inside the National Gallery on St Kilda Road. Stand inside the gallery close to the water wall at the entrance. Be there at [AGREED TIME] today. I will approach you once I'm satisfied that you are alone and I'm sure you are calm."

Response Accepting	**Response Other**
If he accepts the meeting time and place, reinforce the message, then hang up. "Good. I will meet you at [AGREED TIME] this afternoon inside the National Gallery." **Hang up. End.**	*Any other response; any attempt to change the meeting place or time; any excuse for anything else:* "If you cannot meet at [AGREED TIME] at the National Gallery this afternoon, I will ring back another day." *If he still refuses to meet at the specified time and place, end call.* **Disconnection Point.**

*

As I walked to the supermarket to buy a mobile phone, I tried to plan the next stages of Sabasa's path to freedom. It was all moving a little too fast for my liking. I would have preferred that she stayed hiding with me for a few weeks—or, if I'm honest, for a few decades—before we began this scramble to free her from her lunatic ex. While I was never anything but confident when speaking with her, in truth, I had little idea what I was doing. The male brain is far more adept at glib responses than actual planning, but now as I walked through my unremarkable, suburban streets, I began a serious consideration of the tasks ahead of me.

Note to self: need to make note of the male brain's capacity to disregard other operators. Sabasa would have at least as much to do as I would, but I thought of the tasks ahead as 'mine'.

Step 1 – deceive the psychopath into waiting at the National Gallery while we break into his house and recover Sabasa's documents, clothes, and anything else we can carry.

Step 2 – and this is where I was a bit stuck. Was Step 2 – get Sabasa onto a plane to Tasmania to hide in the safe (if mildly bizarre) ashram of Shushan, nee Kevin Ayers? Or was a better Step 2 – arrange to have psychopath arrested, locked up, and plot a continuing domestic heaven with Sabasa? I was leaning towards Step 2(b), but I recognised that I was daydreaming.

Step 2 had to be to get Sabasa to Tasmania for a short while, but that raised the far more difficult question of Step 3: what was Step 3?

Sabasa would only agree to suffer the ashram if she thought there was a reasonable chance that she could return to a safe and normal life. How could I organise that? As I walked to the supermarket, I pondered Step 3.

Step 3 – remove the threat of the psychopath. There are very few ways to remove the threat of a psychopath. One method — which Sabasa had already suggested often enough — was to end his existence. Murder is relatively easy (as evidenced by the borderline morons who commit it), but the really difficult problem is the effective disposal of the body. Traditionally, there are two approaches: 1) Hide it where it can never be found; or, 2) Leave it wherever convenient. Option 1) involves planning, work, and a bit of luck. Option 2 requires that there is nothing to connect you to the body once found. Neither option held much appeal. Was there no other way? What if the ex, admittedly a scary and violent man, was not a psychopath, but just an extremely nasty man who, if it could be shown it was in his best interests, would be willing to leave Sabasa alone? Was there no way to organise things so that, should he bother her again, bang! Locked up for ten years or something?

My experience with violent men was limited. As a rule, I avoid them. It's a good rule. But I have read enough about violent men to know that simple things like court injunctions and apprehended violence orders do little to curtail them. So what else could be done?

Neither the walk to the supermarket, nor the walk back with a $29- mobile phone and a prepaid SIM card, provided any answers beyond the need for me to assess the threat posed by Sabasa's tormentor and then to design Step 3 to suit.

*

Weekend Execution

Can you feel it?

Extract from the unpublished work, 'Masculinear', by Thomas Furphy

If nonsense were a river, one of its most important tributaries would be Men and Emotions. So much nonsense has been written, spoken, sung about Men and Emotions, particularly, the need for men to acknowledge emotions, to 'get in touch with their feelings'.

Men do not experience emotions.

There is simply no point in expecting men to talk about emotions. They don't have them. Women have them.

"I feel angry."

That's a woman.

"I am angry."

That's a man.

The woman experiences the emotion of anger because she is sure that she is not anger. She is more than anger. A man *is* angry. He is the condition of being angry. At that moment he is not anything more than that. So when the analyst asks Denise how she feels about Bradley's continuing infidelities, she is able to claim, rightly and at length, that "I feel angry and hurt and, more than all that, I feel disappointed in Bradley and in myself for believing him, and I feel like such a fool for believing him, but at the same time, I feel angry that he's made me feel that way when he's the one who should be feeling... etc, etc."

No surprise, therefore, when it's Bradley's turn and the analyst asks, "How do you feel when you hear Denise, Bradley?" that the first words out of his mouth are likely to be "I don't know. I guess I feel..."

He *doesn't* know and he *is* guessing.

This is an important and rarely understood manifestation of masculinearity. Whether women are *trained* to feel emotion while men are *trained* to assume an emotion or whether there is some biological mechanism involved hardly matters. That's the way it is.

Success and stress

> *Not cut out for housebreaking. Surprisingly stressful. Bowels still unreliable when thinking of our (now) common adversary. Psychopath. Definite psychopath. Step 3 will need to be extreme.*

The extract from my journal is brief. I suppose I was reluctant to describe our escapade in too much detail in case… No, that wasn't it. I was terrified. And most terrifying of all, it all worked as well as I might have hoped. The plan was, in every way, successful. The consequences were not.

It was barely 10 o'clock on Saturday when I returned with my $29 phone and found Sabasa highly anxious. She was looking through the sheets of our script as if seeking comfort in their flimsy self-assurance.

"We don't have to do this until you're ready," I said, perhaps hopefully. "We can wait a day or two… longer if you need."

"No, let's get on with it. I need to confront him."

I didn't point out to her that the idea was *not* to confront him, but to confound him, but I let it go. I am noted for my sensitive handling of anxious women.

"All right, let's warm up Betsy."

"Betsy?"

Betsy was Norma's car, an immaculate Toyota Tiara, which was kept in the tiny garage at the back. I made a point of driving it gently for an hour or so every month to keep it in running order, but I don't drive much. I have never held a driver's licence myself; so I make a point of taking Norma's driving licence with me, not because I expect a traffic cop to believe I am an eighty six year old woman, but as a talisman. And I have a vague plan that I might claim to have somehow grabbed my mother's licence or something. I still have the car serviced at a local garage—probably the only garage in the

Success and stress

world with original Tiara parts. The owner of the garage bought up all he could find knowing Norma would be a reliable customer for many years. His son is now middle-aged and greets the Tiara like an old friend when I tootle in for a service.

"Betsy is a green, three speed manual Toyota Tiara. A classic."

"Is it reliable?" she asked quickly.

"Betsy is a byword for reliability. She has been in harness since 1963 and has never missed a beat. She has driven nearly 15,000 miles but should be good for another 180,000 if needed. She has led a genteel life."

I knew Betsy's history by rote because Sid, the old mechanic, and more latterly, Geoff, his son, would relate her history to me every time I brought her in.

"Okay. Run me through the plan again."

"The plan is that we drive close to your ex's house and park. You will sit luxurious but inconspicuous in Betsy's very comfortable back seat while I watch the house. From your position in the back, you will call and we will follow the script. Then we wait to see if he takes the bait. As soon as we see him moving, I will drop our leaflets in all the neighbour's letterboxes and stick one to the front of his fence. Then we will stroll into his house, you will remove your belongings, and we will depart."

Sabasa gnawed on her bottom lip. I was astonished again at how entrancing this woman was.

"The neighbours won't have had time to read the leaflets."

"No, I would have preferred to drop them in a day or two before, but just dropping them into letterboxes may give me an opportunity to tell anyone nosing about what we're doing. The one on the front fence should be enough to calm anyone who comes investigating the alarm. But don't worry. No one investigates alarms until they've been going off for hours."

"How much time will we have?"

"It has to take him an hour. It would take him that long to drive to the Gallery and turn around straight away. So it's likely that he'll be gone for an hour and a half, at least. And we won't need more than ten, fifteen minutes."

"You're sure?"

She looked into my eyes, searching for confidence, certainty, knowledge. None of which I had.

"Of course I'm sure. But don't let me rush you if you need more time. We can afford to wait a day or two if you prefer."

"No, let's do it. I want to get him out of my life. I need my documents. What will I carry my stuff in?"

"How much do you think you'll have?"

She thought for a moment. "I can make do with nothing but my purse and passport, but if I can grab some clothes, too, that would be good."

I walked into Norma's bedroom and returned with a medium sized, slightly shabby, faux tweed suitcase.

"Big enough?" I asked.

"Sure, but won't it be conspicuous us carrying something that looks like it should have gone down with the Titanic?"

"No. We have the perfect disguise. In the garage I have several hi-vis, reflective vests. Once we are wearing those, no one will ask any questions. Besides, this," I said, tapping the suitcase, "might well be a tool box."

"With fake crocodile trim, brass fasteners, and a leather handle," she added, sceptically and, I thought, a little unnecessarily.

"Come along. Let me assemble all the things I need and we'll be off."

I still had no jemmy with which to force the door, but I knew that Betsy had a robust little tyre lever in her vinyl-cased toolkit. I hoped that would be enough.

*

Exile

Extract from "Bridge of Generations, the unauthorised biography of Norma Selfe", unpublished

With the disappearance of Joe—Norma never found out if he had been deported or had simply left—Norma suffered three weeks of misery. She was sick with worry. She traipsed around Richmond looking for him. His employer knew nothing. The grocer's wife thought he had been deported. Norma pestered the clerks in the Federal Government building, trying to find information about him, trying to ascertain if he had been deported. She found nothing. There was nothing to suggest he had ever existed. Nothing but the baby, of course. The baby growing inside her before the suspicion of her pregnancy. Growing with the unrelenting vitality of a baby conceived by two young, healthy people.

Norma waited nearly ten weeks before telling her parents. The act of confession was horrible. She watched herself diminish. She changed. She felt the change in their perception of her physically changing her. She was no longer herself. She was contorted with their revulsion into a new self. It was as if her previous years had never been. Her act stole her from her parents. The little girl on the swing, the child tearing bread for the ducks in the Botanical Gardens, the little girl walking bravely to her first day at school. She was gone. Only the whore remained. The whore of the itinerant Italian. She breathed the spores of their disgust into her lungs and felt it infecting her, growing alongside the healthy baby boy.

She was sent away to a lying in boarding house in Horsham, a bleak, pinched, dreary place where several others of her type were waiting. She could remember little about that time: the dreadful food, the work in the laundry, the terrible heat of that dry, country town. The loneliness which grew inside her and announced itself with a single, infant cry one night.

She never saw her baby. She never lost her loneliness. In all her little pocket diaries. All kept in her bedroom. All full of trivial entries. Always a star in red on the same date: 24th September. Every year. Sixty-six little pocket diaries.

© Copyright 2016, Thom Furphy

*

Success and stress

By the early afternoon, we were ready. I had Betsy's tyre lever, a hammer, and a large screwdriver in the suitcase. The hi-vis vests were ready on the floor of the car. Twenty beautifully formatted flyers were printed with the name and logo of a genuine alarm company (pilfered from the internet—add it to my charge sheet) with our agreed text. I had rung Norma's phone a couple of times from the new mobile phone to make sure it was working (and to make sure I knew how to work it).

Sabasa was looking ever more nervous. She was almost hunched with anxiety. She walked to the kitchen and I heard her turn on the tap and sip some water. When she returned, she looked ill. Her golden, Spanish complexion now looked almost grey. Her lips were pressed and pale. I didn't try to make her feel better. I had no idea what fears she was facing. Instead, I affected a cheerful 'busyness' to reassure her. And me. I hadn't done anything like this for a long time[4].

"Righto. 1:30 now. We can be outside his place in half an hour. Let's tell him to meet you at the Gallery at 2:15. That gives him time, but ensures he has to hurry to get there."

"Okay."

She could barely speak.

"Remember the script. If he argues about the time, or can't make it for any reason, you tell him you'll call back in a few days and you hang up, okay?"

"Yes."

"We are not going to do anything that puts us in danger. Our first priority is our safety. If this doesn't work, we'll try something else later."

"Yes. Let's go, Thom. I just want to go."

We left the house by the back door to walk to the garage. As I locked the back door, I cast a wistful glance into my comfortable, safe, little home. It looked so homely and

---

[4] I'm assuming we can all agree that 'ever' is a long time.

complete. It was missing a large, black steel kitchen knife, but I wasn't to know that.

We opened the garage, and I backed Betsy out into the old night soil lane which ran past the back of Norma's backyard. I let Sabasa into the back seat, shut the garage door, and we drove through my comfortable, middle-class suburb of aging family homes gradually being bought up by new families or being renovated into tiny, suburban palaces. We drove through the adjacent, slightly less well-heeled suburb, past shopping centres and schools, past trams and nature strips, past all those other people's pasts and presents. We drove across another suburb, another set of shopping strips, houses, pavements. We were closing on our destination. Sabasa was silent the whole trip, and I was grateful. The consequence of what we were doing was apparent to me, and I didn't like it. I am not an actor. I am an observer. I do not try to engage with the world; I prefer to watch it. But here was I, engaged like Betsy's top, third gear. Like Betsy, I wondered if I shouldn't be back in the garage. At one of the shopping strips I spotted a chemist and pulled over.

"Why are you stopping?"

"Chemist. Going to grab some ear plugs. You wait in the car."

I purchased a couple of sets of foam ear plugs and handed them to Sabasa as I got back in the driver's seat.

We turned into the ex's street and then parked in a street which ran off it at a right angle. I did a u-turn so we were facing the house. It was just as Sabasa had described it: one of a pair of townhouses which had been constructed on the plot of what had once been a small family home. I could see the side gate we would have to force and it didn't look too formidable. I turned to Sabasa in the back seat. She was cowering in the corner, too scared to lift her head to look at the house.

"It's okay. All quiet. The side gate looks easy to me. Are you ready to call him?"

She nodded quickly, but made no attempt to sit up or use the phone which was cradled in her lap.

"Would you like me to call and pass the phone to you?"

She shook her head, but still made no move.

"Tell you what. You sit here for a minute or two; I'll letterbox the adjacent houses. That'll give us a couple of minutes to assess the scene."

Again, she nodded quickly. I took the small sheaf of leaflets and a hi-vis vest. I stepped out of the car, pointedly locking the car door behind me. I put on the hi-vis vest and started dropping leaflets into the eight or ten houses on the opposite side of the road from the ex. There wasn't a person in sight. It was one of those, 'Dad's playing golf and Mum's at the gym on a Saturday' sort of suburbs.

I crossed the road and dropped leaflets in the four houses either side of the ex. I kept a couple of leaflets spare and walked back to Betsy.

Sabasa hadn't moved. I tapped on the window of the passenger side back door, indicating the door lock. Sabasa slid across the bench seat and unlocked the door.

"Okay," I began as I sat down. "Time to make the call if you think you're up to it."

To my surprise, Sabasa sat straight up, brushing some hair away from her face and began dialling the number.

"Put the speaker on," I reminded her.

We both sat listening to the phone ringing. I think we both wanted it to continue ringing without anyone picking up. But he did.

"Hello?" A brusque, male voice. Not deep, but authoritative.

Sabasa was silent for a moment. She had the script in front of her, but for a moment I thought she would be unable to speak.

"Hello?" More peevishly this time.

When Sabasa did speak, I marvelled at her delivery and the control in her voice. She was smooth and calm and careful. She could have been a recording for a call centre's 'Dealing with Difficult Customers' training session.

"It's me. I'm not ringing to discuss anything now, but I want to meet so we can agree how I can recover my possessions."

She was word perfect, and not even looking at the script. I realised she had played this scene many, many times in her head.

Now the ex was silent. I saw Sabasa's lips begin to form a word, but I held my finger to my lips. Wait. We are in control. We wait.

"Is that really you?" he asked finally. I pointed to the next line of the script. She nodded. She was completely in command.

"At some point, we are going to have to talk about what happened, but not now. First, I need to get my possessions out of your house. The only things I want are my clothes and my personal documents. I am not making any claim on anything of yours or anything we bought together."

She concatenated two steps, but she was right. We needed to make this a fast as possible.

"Listen, this doesn't have to be a big drama. Don't you think you're over-reacting?" Ah! The old, male 'let's be reasonable' ploy—the precursor to restating one's position and leading, if ignored, to the variety of temper tantrum preferred by the speaker: sometimes sulking, sometimes storming out, sometimes violence. Sabasa was having none of it. She moved smoothly to the next line in the script.

"I want to meet somewhere public and I want your agreement that there will be no drama. We are meeting to plan how I can pick up my possessions, or how you can deliver them to me if you don't want me in your house. Do you agree?"

"Look, this is stupid. Why don't you just come over now and pick up anything you want? Anything. Take it all."

Success and stress

I pointed to our agreed response, but there was no need. Sabasa was already answering, this time reading from the script.

"I will only discuss how we can meet to agree how I can recover my possessions. If you insist on talking about anything else, I will hang up."

"Fine, but you're making this harder than it needs to be." Silly woman. Why wouldn't you trust a man who has routinely abused you?

"I want to meet inside the National Gallery on St Kilda Road. Stand inside the gallery close to the water wall at the entrance. Be there at quarter past two this afternoon. I will approach you once I'm satisfied that you are alone and I'm sure you are calm."

"Jesus Christ, it's not a fucking spy movie. Which one is the National Gallery? The one with the spire on top?"

For the only time in the conversation, Sabasa deviated from the script.

"Look it up, dickhead. Quarter past two, inside the National Gallery."

He started to speak again, but she hung up at once.

"Brilliant!" I cried. I wanted to hug her, but she instantly slumped down in the seat again, shaking.

"Okay, well done!" I reassured her again. "Now, slip on your hi-vis, but keep low in the seat. I'll get the tools from the boot and we'll watch what he does. Which is his car?"

"The black Audi."

Of course. The one with tinted windows to disguise the fact its driver was, in Sabasa's elegantly precise expression, a dickhead. I stepped out of the car and opened Betsy's boot to retrieve Norma's suitcase. It really didn't look like a toolbox. I may have had a touch of dickhead about myself as well, but there was nothing I could do about it now. I put the suitcase on the nature strip next to the car, opened the passenger side front door and settled down to wait and watch. Sabasa remained hidden in the back seat.

We didn't have long to wait. A few minutes after Sabasa's masterful mic drop phone call, the front door of the ex's house opened and I had my first look at the psychopath.

He was disappointingly ordinary. Admittedly, he looked fit. He was barely taller than average, about my own height, dressed in the uniform of pre-middle-aged men: shirt loosely hanging over his trousers, chinos or some such below-the-waist crime, and trainers. And sunglasses, of course. Perched on top of his neat little haircut, sunglasses which he slipped on as he got into the car. Tinted windows and sunglasses. Can't have too much eye protection.

Dickhead.

I turned to Sabasa. She was still looking sick.

"We have a good hour to get in and out before there is any chance he'll return. So let's work calmly and carefully, and above all, let's look like workmen. Let's be slow."

Sabasa nodded weakly and started to get out of the car. I picked up the couple of spare leaflets I had and told her to wait by the car for a moment while I spoke to the neighbours. I walked to the town house that was the pair of the ex's house and knocked on the door. I could hear activity within and wasn't surprised by the sight of a harassed, young mother who opened the door a few inches while leaning down to restrain a small child.

"Yes?" she asked, exasperated.

"Courtesy call, madam." I intoned sententiously. "We'll be working on the alarm system next door for about twenty minutes." I handed her one of the leaflets. "You may hear the alarm go off briefly a couple of times as we replace the old and test the new one." I smiled ingratiatingly. "We'll do our best to keep the noise down."

"Okay, thanks," she muttered, closing the door and addressing herself to the second pair of footsteps thumping down the hall towards the door, "Enough, Tristan! No running!"

I tried the house on the other side of the ex's, but there was no answer. I walked back to Betsy. Sabasa was standing, wearing her hi-vis vest and holding the suitcase, nervously waiting to start.

"All clear. Let's walk over slowly to the house. You start looking around the front door as if you're looking for the alarm box or fuses or something. I'll go to the side gate."

We starting walking towards the house.

"Remember," I said, turning to her and smiling as if I were actually confident of what we were doing, "we have plenty of time, and if we strike any problems, we pack up carefully and depart. You're okay?"

Sabasa turned a sunny smile to me as if she were a respectful colleague and muttered through her teeth, "Stop asking me if I'm okay, Thom. It's fucking irritating."

It was my turn to nod.

We reached the house and Sabasa walked straight to the front door and began looking around the door frame. She called out to me, "You check the side there! There's no inverter box here."

I was squatting down before the side gate, opening the suitcase and wondered vaguely if an inverter box was a real thing or whether Sabasa was just in character. I inserted the tyre lever below the gate directly beneath the latch. I stood up, leant my weight against the gate and jammed on foot down on the tyre lever. There was a slight splintering sound, but the gate held firm. I tried again, this time thumping my shoulder into the gate as I stamped on the tyre lever. Miraculously, the gate popped open. Sabasa walked around and gave me a quiet look of admiration.

"I didn't think you actually knew how to do that, Thom," she murmured.

"One down. One to go." I muttered in reply, hoping the back door would prove as easy.

I gathered up the suitcase and tyre lever and followed Sabasa down the side of the house to the back door. I propped open the flywire screen door and took a good look at the back door. As she had described, it was an ordinary plywood door. There was a glass panel next to it. I peered around to see if the keys were in the door. They weren't.

"This is where we resort to brute force, I'm afraid. It will be noisy when we get in. Got the ear plugs?"

Sabasa handed me a set and put her own in.

"Where is the alarm box?"

She pulled an ear plug out.

"What?"

"Where is the actual alarm box? When we get in, the first thing we need to do is decommission the alarm."

"Decommission?"

I held up the tyre lever.

"Oh. In the front hall, high on the right hand side near the front door. You'll need a ladder—something to stand on—to reach it. But… "

No need to let a woman finish her sentence. Action!

"Okay, here goes," I rammed the ear plugs into my ears and pushed the spaded end of the tyre lever between the door and the door jamb, next to the lock. I leaned back and yanked at the tyre lever.

It popped out and I staggered backwards.

I hammered it back and tried again, this time putting pressure on the tyre lever before yanking it back. The door frame splintered and the door shifted, but didn't open, but I'd done enough to trigger the alarm. It sounded like an air raid over Berlin. I wriggled the tyre lever in against the lock and tried again. This time, the door came loose and I threw my shoulder against it. It flew open and I stumbled inside. Smooth work, cat.

I regained my balance and ran through the kitchen to the corridor, grabbing a kitchen chair as I went. I placed the chair beneath the alarm which was flashing a blue light and shrieking at the intrusion. I climbed up the chair and began a frenzied thrashing of the alarm with Betsy's tyre lever. For some reason, I remembered the way I'd beaten one of Norma's rugs to clean it after I'd first moved in. There was a lot less dust from the alarm box, but a lot more noise. I jammed the tyre lever under the sheet metal casing and levered it up off the wall. It dangled, shrieking and flashing, hanging from a series of wires. I grabbed the case and jumped off the chair. The alarm came away from its wiring, probably blowing all the fuses in the house, but the alarm was off.

I dropped the alarm box in the hall and pulled the ear plugs out of my ears. Sabasa, who was standing in the hall watching me, did the same.

"Aren't you worried about fingerprints?" she asked, looking at the alarm box on the floor.

"Not at all. Your ex is hardly going to involve the police and risk you spilling the beans on him. Let's get going."

"I told you I knew the code... He uses his mobile number."

I nodded stupidly. She had mentioned that she knew the code. Tried to make a mental note to examine the male preference for violent action over sensible action, but decided this wasn't the time for it. Besides, I quite liked making a mess of his house.

We hurried into the master bedroom and Sabasa began rummaging around in the wardrobe built along one side of the room. I placed the suitcase, opened, on the bed.

"Fill 'er up and let's get moving," I added helpfully.

Sabasa had already found her passport and a purse and threw them into the suitcase. Then she pulled some clothes from the wardrobe and drawers and threw them into the suitcase. She snapped the lid shut and threw the suitcase on the floor.

"We're all done?" I asked.

"Nearly."

Sabasa drew a long, black steel knife from inside her trousers: Norma's carving knife with the bone handle. Before I could utter a word, she began hacking the bed, the pillows, the mattress, hacking and slashing. To describe it accurately, I would first have to change the description of my assault on the alarm box from 'frenzied' to 'surgically precise'.

"Something to remember me by," she muttered grimly at last, stabbing the knife with a final, fierce thrust into the wooden headboard of the bed. Then she reached under the bed and pulled out a rectangular cardboard box. She threw aside the lid and tipped the contents onto the bed. A collection of handcuffs, chains, ropes, a riding crop, and something with an electrical cord tumbled onto the ruined bed.

"Let's go," she breathed, picking up the suitcase and turning to the door. She was exhausted. I gently took the suitcase from her.

I reached behind to the knife still quivering in the bedhead and, with some difficulty, removed it. I had always been fond of that knife, and that fondness had just grown. I clicked open the suitcase and slipped the knife inside. I followed Sabasa out to the kitchen and the back door.

"Nothing else you want?" I asked her.

"Let's just get out of here," she returned, and began heading for the side gate.

"Wait," I called quietly. "Let's leave through the garage. Less conspicuous."

I didn't understand the look on Sabasa's face as I made the suggestion, but I made straight for the garage at the back of the property.

The garage door was flimsy, although the lock on it was better than the house lock. A single kick on the lock and the door burst open. Inside, I instantly understood Sabasa's reaction. The garage was kitted out with a patient table with restraining straps, a rack of canes and whips, a selection of faux leather masks, a ball gag, a camera and professional looking sound equipment. There were shelves of CDs and hard drives.

"Fuck…" It was the only syllable I was capable of uttering.

Sabasa was still standing outside the door.

"I can't go in there again. Let's go out the front."

I hurried out after her.

We walked quickly back to Betsy. All my good intentions about moving slowly were forgotten. We threw the suitcase and tyre lever into the boot, stripped off our hi-vis vests and threw them in, then Sabasa fell into the back seat and I got into the driver's seat and started Betsy. As I was pulling out of kerb, I had a thought. I drove to the lane behind the ex's house and backed up to his garage, leaving Betsy running in neutral.

"What are you doing? Let's get out of here!" Sabasa was close to losing all control.

"Sit still. This won't take a minute. We have time."

I raced around to the front of the house and went through the side gate and into the garage. I opened the electric roller door from inside the garage and then stepped forward and opened Betsy's boot. Her exhaust was popping along unconcernedly.

I went back into the garage and scooped out the contents of the CD and hard disk shelves and threw them into the boot. I returned and yanked the computer which was connected to the camera from its stand, pulling out cables as they got in the way. I took everything that looked as if it might contain data. I threw it all indiscriminately into the boot and slammed it shut.

I shut the roller door from inside the garage, ducking out as it closed. I got in the driver's seat, eased Betsy into first and we rolled away. Sabasa was hidden and silent in the back seat.

An extended breather

> Quiet day spent organising tickets to Hobart. Spoke to Kev about accommodation. Business must be booming; there is one other guest. He reassured me that he'd only be charging 'mates rates'. I told him to take it off the sum he owes me.

I ought to have expected to arrive back at our home on Saturday afternoon in triumphant mood, but we were both too drained, too mentally exhausted. I parked Betsy in the garage, slipped her key back under the driver's floor mat where I kept it because that's where Norma kept it (and where I found it when I first found Betsy). I locked the garage doors by sliding the length of four-by-two across the garage doors and into its iron bracket—a primitive arrangement, but effective—and turned back to see Sabasa climbing slowly out of the back seat.

"Let's get you inside," I urged her, softly. "I'll make a pot of tea and you have a rest."

We walked together into the house. I stepped through to the kitchen; Sabasa went straight into her bedroom.

"I'll bring you tea in a few minutes," I called.

I fussed around in the kitchen making tea and putting a few biscuits on a plate. When the tea was properly drawn, I placed the pot, cups, and plate of biscuits on a tray and carried them to her room.

She was drawn up into a small comma of sadness underneath the bed clothes, fast asleep. I felt a drenching urge to kiss her on the forehead, and even stepped forward to do so, before realising I'd probably tip a trayload of tea things over her if I tried. I turned and walked quietly out of her room. I didn't realise it then, of course, but I would never be closer to kissing her.

An extended breather

I drank my tea and crumbled the biscuits around in my mouth, wondering if I should have a rest myself. I was suddenly exhausted. Instead, as the magic of the tea molecules worked their way through my blood stream, I began planning the next steps. Now that we had Sabasa's documents, we could buy a ticket to Tasmania and she could have a couple of weeks recuperation at Shushan's retreat. First things first: I had to ascertain that the Lotus Enlightenment Centre and Hostel was still operational. I hadn't heard anything from Kevin for some months. I walked over to the Norma's telephone and looked up his number in the small bakelite teledex she had used to keep all her important phone numbers and to which I now added the few numbers I ever needed.

I was relieved to find the ashram was at least still connected when I called it. I waited a few moments before the voice of the mystic seer and spiritual guide, Shushan, answered gently,

"It is a good day."

"Kev, it's me, Thom. Listen, I have a friend who needs to visit the ashram."

"Thom! Great, of course! Are you coming too?"

"Can't make it at the moment, but she needs the full treatment: healthy food, lots of rest, and plenty of meditation work to clear her head. She's had a rough time."

"You know I am always ready to help anyone who needs me." And he was. Kevin was one of life's born helpers. Unfortunately, he was also almost entirely talentless, but Buddhists are big on nothingness, the sameness of the all and the nothing; so a lack of ability to help was never going to stop Kevin from helping. In Kevin's mind 'lack' was the same as 'superfluity'.

"How are you off for funds at the ashram?"

"Oh, well, we're pretty well self-sufficient, you know," he began modestly and with a total disregard for the truth.

"Can I put a couple of hundred into your account to help?"

"Donations are always welcome, of course."

"I'll put it in tonight. Her name is Sabasa. I'm buying a ticket for her now. As soon as I know when her flight gets in, I'll call to let you know. Make sure you feed her well—that's why I'm donating the money—and give her plenty of time to herself if she needs it."

"She will come back a new woman."

"No doubt. Is there anyone else staying with you?"

"Only one other who's booked in for a couple of weeks yet. She's making great progress. She's exploring massage and reiki healing. Recovering from a bad relationship. Fiona."

I was ashamed to find I was relieved that there were no men at the ashram. It would have been just my luck to find it full of buff, Tasmanian conservation workers taking a break from saving small, fluffy creatures. Kevin himself was no threat. Although an enthusiastic admirer of the feminine in all ways, Kevin tended to envelope any human contact in such a thick blanket of mystical and spiritual significance that most woman were unaware that his earnest invitations to engage in solemn and tedious rituals were meant as a precursor to romantic involvement. He did ensnare his share of trippy, airheads, of course, but I couldn't see Sabasa succumbing.

"Okay. I'll call you when I've got a flight. Can you pick her up at the airport?"

"Fiona has a car and is happy to let me use it; so no problem."

It sounded as though Kevin might have Fiona lined up for a few spiritual alignment rituals.

"Thanks. I'll call soon with the flight info."

"Sure you wouldn't like to come as well? You could relax, help me with a couple of jobs here?"

"Next time. Things to do here."

"Only material things. You need to free yourself."

Yes, but I like material things. I poured another cup of Darjeeling into one of Norma's fine bone china teacups and smelt its gentle, astringent aroma. I am a very material being. I found a flight for Sabasa for Sunday around midday, but before I made the booking I needed her details. I fished her passport out of the suitcase and learned her real name. Her surname was disappointingly anglo. Her given name was Claire. Pretty. It suited her. She remains Sabasa to me, of course. I made the booking, and then made sure Shushan would be there to pick her up. I thought about doing some work on one of my projects, but found I was just too weary. I transferred three hundred dollars into Shushan's account and then headed off to bed for a quick nap. I didn't wake for fifteen hours.

*

The difficult problem of women in Parliament

Extract from A Programme of Moderate Political Reform in Australia, www.pmpra.com

How might a truly representative parliament be stocked with true representatives? We have lived long enough with the duplicity of a party system which only delivers representative democracy infrequently and by accidental coincidence of party interests and the repayment of political favours with the interests of the population. If you need proof of how unrepresentative and corrupt the current system is, consider the—for some reason—vexing issue of 'Women in Parliament'. This is always presented as a serious issue that requires a great deal of effort and one which our major political parties have been grappling with for decades.

Huh?

Isn't this a 'serious issue' you could resolve pretty much instantly? If a party were short of women parliamentarians , couldn't that party say, "Next election, we will be standing women in ALL the safe seats, until we have parity of gender representation."

Yes they could. Or they could address the issue in any one of a dozen other ways. But that would mean they cared to do so. And they don't. Political parties will never do anything—even if it's in the national interest to do so—if it contravenes the interests of the party.

An extended breather

And gender disparity is only the most obvious example of the unrepresentativeness of our current parliaments. Once you start looking at age, race, education, sexuality, you see more and more problems.

I have already suggested that the parliament should be populated in much the same way as our juries—by random selection—and in broad outline, this is true, but the selection of parliamentary representatives requires more than a reliance on random selection. After all, with a mere 150 parliamentarians in our current federal lower house, it would be very likely that a random selection of the population would result in a parliament with no or little representation of rural Australia, for example. It could also result in the same sort of gender inequalities being inflicted on our parliament: one term many more women; next term many more men.

So while the selection of parliamentarians must include a free and random selection of candidates, there must be some selectivity about the pools of candidates for each seat.

The first thing I would like to suggest is an immediate doubling of the number of parliamentarians. Unpopular, I know. But hear me out. Each seat should have two parliamentarians: one male; one female. This instantly resolves our issues with gender disparity. We select our candidates for each seat from two pools within the electorate: a male pool and a female pool. What of those people who don't identify as one gender or the other? Those people may be placed in both pools. This may mean a very tiny increase in the representation of those who don't identify as male or female, but given their complete absence from representation in the past, we have a bit of making up to do anyway.

Every adult citizen should be required to be available for parliamentary duties once. Unlike jury selection, a stint as a parliamentarian should preclude you from any future involvement in parliament. Of course, there will be people who may be excused from duty on medical, psychological, or personal grounds, but these exceptions are common to all forms of mandatory service. We had them for National Service; we have them for jury duty. These will not be difficult to define.

© Copyright 2016, Thom Furphy

Farewell and a chance to say hello

> *Spoke to S re the spiritual side of the retreat. She didn't want him warned off; so I suspect she will be bombarded with a lot of nonsense about energy and cleansing and alignment. Will probably do her good. She needs to immerse herself in a different madness. Got tickets and drove her to the airport.*
>
> *Strangely empty house on my return. I have always felt at home here. I have always felt comfortable sharing it with Norma and her past. Now it feels empty for the first time. Must explore the masculine need for inert companionship.*
>
> *Strange meeting of an 'other' self. To look into one's own (if alternative self's) eyes and see deadness. Should examine the tiny divergences which create apparently entirely different masculine selves. I have a name for my other.*

Sunday morning was an early breakfast. We both woke early and we both woke hungry. Strangely, neither of us spoke about our successful house breaking exercise of the previous day. We simply started talking about the next steps. As we sat down together to our porridge and tea—I insisted that this was no morning for coffee, despite Sabasa's begging for coffee; tea is restorative, I reminded her, coffee is additive, and we needed restoring—we discussed the next steps of our plan. Initially, Sabasa needed convincing again that a rest cure in Tasmania was what was required.

"Why don't I just get out of Melbourne now and head to Sydney?" she asked. "Now that I've got my ID and some clothes I can escape for good."

"That's the whole point. You need to escape for good, not for now. You are having a proper rest. Proper time to think, plan, resolve the next phase of your life. You need to be free to live anywhere, to move wherever you like. Escaping for good means regaining control. We have to eliminate any threat to you from your ex."

"How am I going to do that?"

"I'm not going to pretend I know yet, but the first thing you are going to do is to relax. Nothing goes away in the meantime. You can still go to Sydney. You can still disappear to Western Australia, if you want. But you have to give yourself time and space to think this through. The fight/flight response is great for getting you out of immediate danger. We've done that. But it's a terrible way to determine the next eighty years of your life. Please trust me on this. The ashram is the safest place in world. The CIA couldn't find you there. The only danger is that you start believing some of the religious teachings of Shushan. Incidentally, we should speak about that."

"What? Religion?"

"Yes, you're not susceptible to spiritual nonsense, are you?"

"What do you mean? God and stuff?"

"God and stuff. Universal plans. Zen. Kevin is big on wholeness. You'll have to put up with conversation peppered with wholeness."

"Is this a cult, Thom? I'm not letting myself be controlled by anyone again," she added fiercely.

Remembering the dismemberment of the ex's bed, I believed her.

"There is nothing remotely cult-like about Kevin or his ashram. Kevin is a well-meaning, gentle soul who is genuinely concerned to help people discover their path in life. Kevin could no more look to control you than he could put together a coherent summary of his philosophy. Trust me, you are entirely safe with Shushan, as long as you're not infuriated by the placid patchwork of spiritual scraps he has stitched together. He thinks of it as a quilt of ideas. To the rest of us it looks like a ragbag."

"No, that's all right. Will he leave me alone if I need it?"

"Sabasa," I looked into her deep, chocolate eyes, "I wouldn't recommend this for you if I didn't believe it was right. Kevin is a gentle lunatic, but he is caring and kind. And believe me, you are more than a match for him intellectually. The rest of the world regards him as a useless dreamer, which he is, but even the useless have their uses. I think Milton said that."

"I just don't see the point, exactly. What will have changed by the time I get back?"

"Probably nothing," I replied, little realising just how wrong I was to be, "but you will have had a chance to think things through carefully, as will I. We will compare plans when you're back and whatever you decide to do, I will help you do it. The main thing is to get you somewhere safe for a little while. It will allow the ex to blow off steam and if he knocks himself out looking for you in Melbourne or Sydney, so much the better. We are doing this to get you back in control of your life."

A rash promise, but I believed it.

Sabasa hadn't managed to save many clothes, but what she had, she packed, along with the clothes I had bought her and a few toiletries. I handed her some cash which she took reluctantly.

"I've got my cards back now. I don't need money from you."

"You haven't checked your accounts yet," I reminded her. "For all you know, there's nothing in there. I wouldn't put it past the bastard to have emptied your accounts."

Apparently, neither did she, because she took the money quietly and folded it into her purse.

"I'm keeping track of all this," she added quietly.

"I know. And look, you probably won't need any money at all. There's nothing to buy on the ashram unless Kevin's got around to printing any of his books. But you might need a taxi or something."

Farewell and a chance to say hello

"Can I take the mobile phone?" she asked.

The mobile phone was the only thing the ex had to connect her to the house breaking. I had switched it off as soon as we had got back and I wasn't in any hurry to switch it back on again.

"No. I may need that. Kevin's got a phone if you need to call me, but you're there to rest; so send me a postcard. Or better still, observe radio silence until I contact you."

Late that morning, we took a cab to the airport. I didn't drive Betsy because somewhere in the back of my mind was a warning to keep her off the streets. She is a distinctive car and I wanted her tucked up safely in the garage out of sight of any lunatic ex cruising past. I never told Sabasa my fears, but I had thought often enough about it. This house was the last place the ex knew of anyone seeing Sabasa and he was likely to give the area at least a cursory examination if he hadn't already.

I saw Sabasa through to the departure gates with a final reminder of how to contact Shushan if he wasn't at the airport and made sure she had Norma's number to contact me if she needed anything. We had agreed on a fortnight's stay, but if she was enjoying the peace and quiet, she might stay longer.

I took a bus and tram back to Norma's rather than a taxi because I routinely try to save money and I wanted some time to think. Why I should think better on a bus and tram than sitting comfortably at home isn't clear to me now, and I couldn't have explained it then. But that's what I did.

Strangely, I didn't think about anything much except how much I loved having Sabasa in my life. I was without her for less than two hours by the time I walked in the front door and I was already lonely. It was a strange feeling. I like being alone. I like being an observer rather than an actor. But now it appeared that I liked living with a beautiful, dark-haired Spanish woman whose voice had lost every trace of its accent, but which thrilled me with every syllable it uttered, which thrilled me, even in memory.

I made tea, but without thinking, I made enough for two. For so long, I had, several times a day, made myself a pot of tea. Now, after a few days, I was making tea for two. Ridiculous. To encourage myself to get over the loneliness, I tried to concentrate on creating a sensible list of the tasks I hoped to complete while Sabasa was in Tasmania. I sat at the kitchen table with a pen and my shopping list pad and began the list. For some reason, the first task I thought of was my need to visit Dr No at his practice to 'pick up my results' and start my, doubtless, expensive psychotherapy sessions with him. Did I really need to see him? Recent events had taken my mind off any other troubles and I hadn't been able to give any thought or worry to the now permanent absence of morning erections, but, shameful as it is now to admit, I wanted to ensure that should Sabasa come back into my life as more than just a housemate, I would be ready to engage as an enthusiastic and satisfactory partner.

I wrote: 1. Make appt with Dr No.

Next, I thought of Betsy with her bootload of pornography, or whatever filth Sabasa's ex had collected on all the CDs and hard drives. What should I do with it? It might be evidence. It might contain such disgusting images of Sabasa that I didn't want to risk looking at it. Interesting verb: risk. What was I scared of? Betraying her by seeing it? Having her feel ashamed that I had seen it? Enjoying it?

I was already uncomfortably aware that there were echoes of similarity between me and her ex. We were both besotted—in very different ways, it's true, but we were clearly both besotted. We both wanted her in our lives. We both enjoyed feeling we had some control of her life. In my own mild—did I dare call it sexless?—way, I was trying to control her, to keep her. I was aware of the desire and I was suspicious of it.

In the end, I resolved to trust myself. I wrote: 2. Review contents of boot. Then, 3. Destroy all superfluous material. 4. Decide what to do with remaining material.

That was enough consideration of the things in Betsy's boot. I felt unclean just thinking about it. What else did I need to do? I try to find six things to make a list. Anything less is a lost.

I wrote, 5. Resolve the psycho dilemma, and, 6. Decide how much to involve Sabasa in the decision.

This was a pretty feeble 5 and 6, admittedly, and hardly needed to be included on the list as they were occupying most of my conscious and probably all my subconscious thought, but they were important. I had to decide how I could make Sabasa's life free of her psycho and I then had to decide whether to risk involving Sabasa in the decision, particularly if I came down on the side of one of the more drastic choices. Women are notoriously reticent to kill, and despite Sabasa's repeated declarations, I doubted she would follow through if push came to shiv.

I had my list. I had my tea. I decided to start at the top. No point calling for an appointment at Dr No's practice on Sunday. Numbers two, three, and four were too grisly to think about at the moment. That meant the top was 5: how to eliminate the psycho.

There was a firm rapping on the front door.

I lowered my tea cup and walked slowly to the front door. I don't get many visitors, as I think I've already mentioned, and I enjoy their absence.

Norma's house was too old-fashioned to be equipped with a peep hole or even a chain on the door. In Norma's time, one threw the door open to see who was there: Ah! The Rawleigh's man! Is it March already?

I opened the front door. Not the Rawleigh's man, a policeman. Now, had this happened a year or two ago, I might have felt nervous. I half expected someone to initiate enquiries about Norma, but by now I was quite secure in my possession of the house. I hadn't finalised the transfer of the title, it's true, but I had full power of attorney for Norma.

Farewell and a chance to say hello

"Can I help you?" I asked, politely.

I was looking into the eyes of a younger man, of my height and general build, although he clearly took more fastidious care of his body than I ever had. Nonetheless, the impression I had was of looking into a mirror which took between five and ten years to return a reflection and which showed me the me I might have been if I took an interest in sports, voted Nazi, and lost four fifths of my IQ points.

"Sorry to disturb you sir," he began, his voice had notes of my own. He must have grown up north of Victoria. "We are seeking information from the public about a missing woman."

For a moment, I thought he might be talking about Norma, but he drew a photocopy of a photograph of Sabasa from a manila folder he was carrying.

"She was reported missing about a week ago and we're concerned to find her."

I looked at the image of the woman I had fallen in love with and shook my head slowly. Was it only a week?

"I don't think…" As I spoke, I remembered a dark shape on that night that Sabasa had appeared at my door, frightened, beautiful, alone. The voice that growled at me, could it have been the same voice? I looked back up at the policeman, stared into my own face on top of my own body, but younger, stronger, meaner, stupider.

"I wonder…" I finished weakly.

"Yes," he asked, eagerly. "She was last seen in this street. Do you think you've seen her?" His voice took on an edge of threat. "Your co-operation is very important."

I made a pretence of studying the photo more closely.

"I think I may have seen a woman like her at the supermarket, the little one down the road. How tall is she? She sounded Spanish."

He lost interest immediately.

"She isn't Spanish. She's Australian. One hundred and seventy five centimetres tall. Slim build."

"No accent?" I asked hopefully.

"No accent. Aussie accent. All right, thank you, sir."

"Sorry I couldn't be more help. Can I keep the photo in case I see her? I could call Crime Stoppers…"

"No, that's all right. I've only got this one. Best if you call me directly if you see her. It's a family matter. Her family is very worried." He pulled a business card out of his pocket, a standard police issue card, but wrote his mobile number on it.

"Call me directly if you see anyone you think might be her."

"Will do," I promised smartly, the most helpful Joe Public this cop had seen in a while. "Would you like a cup of tea before you go?" I asked, smiling winningly.

"No thanks," his face betrayed a hint of disgust, imagining I might be propositioning him. "I've got the rest of the street to do."

"Good luck," I wished him as I shut the door.

Was I sure? I was sure. When did Plod ever come singly? When did they ask about a missing person with only one copy of a picture? When did they concern themselves with someone who'd been missing less than a fortnight?

I had a sudden thought that he might be suspicious, but I watched him dutifully knocking at next door's. No, the sod was going up and down my street, hoping to find someone who'd seen her. Well, good luck, you prick.

I had one last test to make. I fished out the mobile phone Sabasa had used to call him, turned it on and checked the phone history. The mobile number he had written on his card was the only number we'd called. There were also 12 missed calls, all from him. I turned the phone off again.

I had met the psycho.

I sat back down at the kitchen table and returned to my list, thinking it was perhaps a good thing that he hadn't accepted the offer of a cup of tea, as I had a list with the following items:

1. Make appt with Dr No.
2. Review contents of boot.
3. Destroy all superfluous material.
4. Decide what to do with remaining material.
5. Resolve the psycho dilemma.
6. Decide how much to involve Sabasa in the decision.

True, he knew Sabasa by a different name, nonetheless, the list might have piqued his policeman's instincts. I looked at his card again. Senior Constable Scott Crennan, his station address and contact numbers, and his handwritten mobile number. Senior Constable meant he was probably no star officer, but there was no doubt that his being a policeman altered my options for '5. Resolve the psycho dilemma'. At the back of my mind had always been the option that we could hold the threat of 'going to the cops' over his head. This now seemed a less effective threat. It also meant that, while he wasn't high enough up the chain of command to be able to involve other police or fabricate evidence against us, it presumably did give him access to police information systems which might make finding Sabasa easier. I also became uncomfortably aware of material in the boot of Betsy. It implicated me in a burglary and, depending on what jolly material Senior Constable Crennan liked to collect, I might well be harbouring a stash of very illegal pornography. There was the mild consolation that a great deal of the material might also implicate the Senior Constable, but the thought of sharing a cell with Scott, a younger, harder version of myself, didn't appeal.

I made the thoroughly distasteful decision to catalogue the Crennan Collection and dispose of anything I didn't need.

Catalogue of disgust

> I need a bath.

It took me several days to begin the task of examining the digital evidence of Crennan's hobby. I found a logical excuse in thinking that I should allow time between his visit and anything I might then decide to do. I reasoned that I should follow my own advice to Sabasa and allow myself time to think before blundering into action. In reality, of course, I was just too nervous to begin. As it happens, I had cause to be nervous. My journal entry following my initial perusal of the material that entertained Crennan was the only record of his activities which I cared to make.

Norma's house has a small room near the back garden which may originally have been a maid's room. It is largely unused and has become a store room for things which don't fit anywhere else. It was into this room that I had lugged all the various bits and pieces I had swept up in my rapid clearing out of Crennan's garage. The plunder included a computer, but no monitor, keyboard, or cables; so I took a few days assembling the missing components in raids on the local pawn shops. It was four or five days after my visit from Senior Constable Crennan that I finally switched on his computer and waited while it booted up.

The password screen appeared. Password protected. Of course it was. I didn't know him well enough to begin to start guessing what he might use as a password. Sabasa might know, or be able to guess, but I had carefully made sure she was out of contact.

Sabasa might know. Think, male brain! Think!

She had known the code for alarm. What had she said? He uses his mobile number. I went back to the kitchen to retrieve Senior Constable Crennan's card. Was it possible that he was handing out the password to his computer in his own handwriting on his own business card?

Q: Who would be that stupid?

A: Senior Constable Scott Crennan.

As the computer came to life, the thought struck me that I probably also had the password or PIN for all Crennan's various electronic accounts. I put that to the back of my mind, but I promised to return to it.

The first surprise was the computer was running Linux. I had Crennan down as a standard Windows man. Linux suggested slightly more computer knowledge than I'd suspected. I took a deep breath and began hunting through the files to see what amused Crennan in his playtime activities in his garage.

I didn't have far to look. Senior Constable Crennan was a disciplined computer user. I would shortly discover just how much he enjoyed discipline. His files were logically arranged and categorised. Somewhere in here he probably ran a database which allowed him to sort and store files based on victim, type of perversion, degree of humiliation, and so on. That's what I would have done, I realised with a creeping disgust. I didn't want to look too closely. He had a large number of folders labelled with the names of women. One of them was Claire. I didn't look at any of his Claire files, but I opened some of the other victims' files. And stopped very quickly. I just needed to understand what he collected. He collected violent humiliation of women.

I looked briefly at some of the CDs and hard drives I'd taken as well. Some were the raw material from which he winnowed the collection he kept on the computer. Some were items of interest he'd collected from fellow perverts on the internet. As soon as I knew that the crème-de-la-crème of his collection was on the computer, I began tossing all the other material into one of the boxes for permanent destruction. I didn't open anything labelled 'Under'. I also had no idea how I could dispose of it. I lugged the box back to the garage and locked it in Betsy's boot while I thought of how to get rid of it. I decided to leave the computer in the spare room, taking care to reset Crennan's password to something secure.

I needed to think about something else. Reviewing a fraction of Crennan's material, even at high speed had left me feeling sick. I needed to talk to someone alive. I decided to call Kevin at the ashram and check that Sabasa was settled in and happy.

Norma's telephone sat on a 1960's, Danish teak telephone table. These once fashionable, low tables had enough room for a telephone, a teledex, and a pad. They had a built in seat at which a lady could decorously sit, dial her friends, and chat about lady things, jotting down notes or appointments as needed. Norma's telephone table had a black vinyl leatherette seat with an upholstered yellow pillow for the back. It was probably selected for the Richmond colours. I sat at the table, looked up Kevin's number in the teledex, and doodled on the pad as I waited for an answer, the perfect Danish husmor.

"It is a good day."

"Kevin? It's Thom, here. I was just ringing about Sabasa. Checking she was okay."

"Great. She's great. Arrived and settling in. Thanks for sending her my way. She's a babe!"

"Buddhists should use the word 'babe' like that. She's there for rest, recovery, and then a bit more rest, okay?"

"No worries. She'll be fine. Rest, recovery, rediscovery. That's the motto here. Would you like to talk to her? She's just in the pod at the moment."

"Sure. If she's free." The pod was a circular room in a mud brick building which served as the central meeting point of the ashram. It was a combination of lounge area, library, and reading room. It was surprisingly beautiful inside. A bench ran all around the room, laden with plush cushions. There were leadlight windows set into the walls around the building, a reminder of the short period when Kevin was partnered with a talented glass artist. She had left to further her artistic horizons with a surfer who'd stayed at the ashram for free in exchange for odd jobs and Kevin's girlfriend. I waited while Kevin went to fetch Sabasa.

"Hello, Thom?" Her voice was the warmth of sunlight through glass on my face. "Is everything okay?"

"Sab. How are you? Just wanted to make sure you were okay. Everything's fine here." I wasn't going to tell her yet about my visit from Crennan.

"No, it's wonderful. It's pretty basic, as you said, but it's so beautiful. And Shushan is lovely, as you promised. And there's only one other person here at the moment. She's really fun. Shushan tells me she has a wonderful, strong aura. And she's wise, he says. Wise with the wisdom of the feminine." She laughed and the sunlight hit rippled water and danced through my heart.

"That's great. You concentrate on resting and thinking."

"Thom, thank you. I want you to know. I feel like I'm breathing. Really breathing again for the first time in so long. Thank you, Thom. You are a wonderful friend."

"You're just saying that because it's true." I dismissed her compliments with the bluff bluster of the stupid male. "I'm pleased you're enjoying it, but remember, we have a lot to do yet to get you truly free."

"I know. But Thom, for the first time, I really believe I can be free again. So thank you."

The phone call wound its way through several more awkward sentences before I hung up, promising to call in a couple of days' time. I don't know if the call did anything for Sabasa, but it worked for me. It cleared my mind of the filth I'd forced myself to witness and it reminded me that this was worthwhile.

I made myself a pot of tea—a Pu Erh—and sat down at my computer to work on one of my projects for an hour or so.

Catalogue of disgust

*

Let's do it! Action as antidote to cognition

Extract from the unpublished work, 'Masculinear', by Thomas Furphy

The male brain is peculiarly constructed to place a high value on action and to regard thought, consideration, evaluation as synonyms for procrastination, or worse, as the same as doing nothing at all. There is a commonly held belief that it is better to 'do something' than to do nothing and even if the doing of the something results in a poor outcome, it will, at least, have 'forced the issue': the clear implication being that a) force is a good thing; and, b) the result of 'the issue' was somehow predetermined and couldn't have been resolved any other way. All of which reinforces the idea that there was no point in thinking about it because you couldn't have thought of any better solution.

For many men, of course, this is true. So inadequate are their powers of reasoning, so stunted is their experience of their intellect, that it is likely that, faced with the simplest of problems, they could never come up with anything more inventive than hitting it with a mallet. Our society bears much of the responsibility for this male inadequacy: many more men would be capable of reason if we placed more value on the teaching and practice of it. Much of the responsibility, but not all. Some men will always reach for the mallet. You can't blame society for genetics.

The purpose of this book is to suggest to men that, if you are not naturally an inveterate malleteer, you might like to consider whether you would benefit from employing your imaginations to better effect when faced with problems. I hope it is clear to you all that alcohol is a mallet, a firearm is a mallet, hitting someone (with or without a mallet) is a mallet.

The next time you hear yourself utter the words or thought, "I may as well just do it", or "Let's just get it over with", I hope you will pause and think "Put down the mallet!" Or, if that isn't possible, take up croquet and put your mallet to socially acceptable use.

*

My own male brain became engaged in thinking about how to dispose of a bootful of binary pornography. I reasoned that, even if I wanted to use this material to disgrace and convict

Crennan, there was more than enough on his computer. Then I reasoned a little further and imagined a barrister questioning me in court.

"So you stole a computer from the garage of my client and took it home with you. Have we established that?"

"Yes, because I knew…"

"Let's stick to the facts and leave speculation about what you 'knew' and when you knew it, shall we? You stole a computer from my client?"

"Yes."

"You then hacked into his computer in order to do what? To look for his financial records?"

"No, I thought, I *knew* he used the computer to record pornography."

"You knew? How?"

"I saw the setup in the garage! The cameras, the table…"

"And you knew, instantly, that it must be being used to record pornography… and remarkably, after having stolen the Senior Constable's computer and hacked into it, you 'found' exactly the sort of pornography you expected."

"Yes, as soon as I had confirmed it contained pornography, I shut the computer down."

"And went straight to the police, I presume?"

"No, I wanted…"

"How long was the computer in your possession before you bothered to inform the authorities, Mr Furphy?"

And then, Crennan's barrister would 'establish' that the time between our raid on Crennan and whenever I turned in the evidence was more than enough time for me to load his computer with anything I cared to find on the dark web, and was I motivated by an interest in Crennan's girlfriend? and so on, and so on.

Catalogue of disgust

I began to think, with some reluctance, that I either turned everything over to the police immediately, or I gave up on the idea that there was any way to use the pornography against Crennan. There was probably some material with Crennan playing a leading role, which would be hard for him to explain, but I couldn't be sure of that without trolling through more of his handiwork and I had no stomach for that. All this thinking was getting me nowhere, so I took another favourite male approach and decided to leave that problem and consider another, simpler problem: how to dispose of the Crennan collection of pornography.

My primitive male brain went first to fire. Burn it all. Did CDs burn? I wasn't sure. They'd probably emit plumes of toxic smoke which might excite the interest of the neighbours. Seeing me standing over a bonfire of CDs and computer hard drives might give rise to further speculation or enquiry, and I have made a point of remaining politely unobtrusive for my neighbours' comfort. It's politic if you're occupying someone else's house.

I realised that what I had to do was clean each and every CD and hard drive, not just delete files, but overwrite and reformat each and every one. It would probably take hours to do it, but I had no choice. Once I was convinced that I had wiped them clean, I would dump them all in a charity bin or, more dramatically, perhaps, I could dump them over Crennan's front porch...

*

Return to Richmond

Extract from "Bridge of Generations, the unauthorised biography of Norma Selfe", unpublished

Norma expected to leave Horsham as soon as she was able, to return to Melbourne and to try to remake her life, but after the birth and adoption of her child, her determination failed. During her lying in, she had been troubled by toothache and had several times been treated by a local dentist, Dr Fong. Although Dr Fong had trained in the Glasgow Dental Hospital, he struggled to attract patients in country Victoria where ching-chong-chinamen were still regarded as suitable only for market gardening and abuse; so he charged very reasonable rates and took patients wherever he could find them.

Norma had enormous respect for Clarence Fong. He had treated her with skill and compassion, despite working alone in a small surgery attached to the side of his weatherboard house. When she had recovered from the childbirth, she approached him for a job, suggesting that she could help him both as a dental nurse and receptionist. Clarence made clear to her that his practice was hardly able to support him alone and he couldn't afford to pay wages. Norma, however, suggested that she could perhaps be engaged as his live-in housekeeper as well, and that way she could also spend time learning her new trade. As long as he provided board, she was happy to stay and work with him.

Clarence could hardly say no. He was aware of her background, of course, and although he worried that it might cause scandal amongst the burghers of Horsham, at least he wouldn't be accused of leading a virtuous white woman astray. Norma was a proven slut. For Norma, who knew that a white woman working for a chow would be considered only one better than sleeping with the blacks under the ironbarks on the reserve, didn't care. She now wore her shame as armour and she had no intention of living to any expectations but her own.

The years she spent with Clarence Fong were some of the happiest and most restful of her life. The ache of missing her child, the ache of longing for her Joe, so painful and distracting in her first years, gradually settled to a long, dark sunset of feelings which she carried with her but which didn't prevent her learning household management, bookkeeping, dental nursing, and ultimately becoming, at Clarence's suggestion and expense, a dental technician, skilled in the making and fitting of dental appliances. In 1960, she won the National Dental Technician's Award for Excellence in Dental Prosthetics. The same year, she moved back to Melbourne to live in her parents' house and look after her mother, her father having died some years before.

© Copyright 2016, Thom Furphy

*

Catalogue of disgust

> Repetition is the mother of invention. Unfortunately, it still requires intellect to father it. Repetition is usually the mother of some very stupid ideas. Particularly when alcohol is the father. The psycho has seen Betsy.

I bought myself a good bottle of whisky and set about cleaning all the writable CDs and hard drives. There was probably some smart way to do it, but I didn't know what it was. I hooked up each drive and typed in the same `shred` command. No doubt there are more secure ways to destroy evidence on a hard disk, but `shred` would be fine for my purposes. I wasn't expecting I'd have to deal with the CIA or MI5; I just wanted to be able to dump the disks and not let Joe Public find Crennan's study material. I couldn't think of any fast way to do it; so I set myself down, and drank a nip whenever the time was passing too slowly. I took great care to keep the cleaned material separate in a new box.

By the time I was finished, I had a box full of blank CDs, DVDs, flash drives, and hard drives and a skinful of fine, malt whisky. I put the box into Betsy's boot, still imagining I would find a charity bin to dump them in, but I returned to the house to pick up the mobile phone and Crennan's business card, neither of which I needed in order to find a charity bin.

I decanted myself into Betsy and drove over to Crennan's house. I parked directly in front of his house, pulled out the mobile phone and checked the business card. Then I called his station.

"Superintendent Crennan, please." I commanded the voice which answered.

"Pardon me?"

"Senior Constable Crennan, please."

"Hold on a moment…" The voice called out to others in the station for Crennan before relaying the news to me. "I think he's just left. Can I help you?"

"No thanks. Personal matter." I hung up. 'Just left' gave me plenty of time. I got out of the car, opened the boot, and took out the carton. I strolled through the front gate and up to Crennan's front door and emptied the carton over his dinky little porch. I returned to Betsy and put the empty carton back in the boot. Flushed with bravado, success, and whisky, I turned the ignition key and checked my mirrors for oncoming traffic before indicating to leave the kerbside (as per driving instruction manual). As I did, I noticed in the rear view mirror a senior constable walking up the street not far from the boundary of his neighbour's property.

I threw the car into gear and drove off hurriedly, now just feeling like something that ought to be flushed.

Had he seen the number plate? Did he know enough about cars to know a Toyota Tiara when he saw one? Had he seen me?

I turned the first corner I could and drove home, locking Betsy in the garage and then scuttled inside. I needed to plan my defences.

The best form of defence

> Not being attacked is the best form of defence. The only useful thing I learnt at school was how to avoid making yourself a worthwhile target. Nothing smart attacks a porcupine. If you know you are going to be attacked, however, don't rattle your quills too loudly. Let the predator walk right into them.

Back in the sanctuary of Norma's comfortable house, I reflected on what had just happened. When I left Norma's, I was pleasantly sozzled with the whisky I'd consumed. The sight of a puzzled looking Senior Constable Crennan in my rear view mirror had sobered me instantly. If he hadn't seen the number plate, I had nothing to worry about. Even if he suspected me, I could likely brazen out a denial. If he had seen the number plate, however, I was in trouble. There were three reasons to suspect that he had seen the number plate:

1. He was a policeman and presumably noticed these sort of things as a habit;
2. I was pulling out from the kerb just as he was arriving and he may even have seen me walking out through his gate;
3. Betsy had been continuously registered since her purchase in 1962 and still had her original, black and white number plates. These are now rare enough for many people to notice.

I decided to work on the assumption that Crennan had seen the plates and to hope that he hadn't. That meant I might have less than thirty minutes before I could expect a visit from a very angry, possibly dangerous young man. I walked through the house, checking for anything which might betray Sabasa's presence. There was nothing obvious. The only thing which connected me to the break in was Crennan's computer, sitting in the back room. I disconnected it from its pawnshop monitor and keyboard and picked it up and walked out the back door. I knew exactly where I was going to hide it: in the same place I had hidden for three nights when I first came to Norma's house.

I walked along the side of the house until I came to the small wooden gate fastened with a slide bolt: the entrance to the crawl space beneath the house. Because the block had a gentle slope from the back to the front, there was not much room when you entered the gate, but as you crawled forward, it became progressively roomier. There wasn't standing room, or anything like it, but it was relatively easy to move around. I knew from my first visit to the house that it was dry under there and there was a roll of old carpet and another roll of underfelt which had been stored there for the past couple of decades. The carpet was still partially unrolled where I had spread it out to sleep on. I pushed the computer hard up against the carpet roll and rolled it forward over the computer. No one looking in would see anything but old carpet.

I contemplated staying under the house but rejected the notion at once. I have always believed it is safer to hide in full view than to attempt concealment. I backed out carefully and pushed the slide bolt shut. I gave myself a good dusting down, resolving to examine myself inside in the light to make sure there were no telltale signs of dust or dirt.

Once inside and once I had brushed away a couple of cobwebs, I put the front porch light on. The front door was locked, and I considered unlocking it or even leaving it open but rejected that thought. Crennan would try to surprise me. He'd be likely to come to the back of the house to try the back door. I made sure the back door was unlocked, turned on all the lights at the back of the house—there was no point in having him damage anything unnecessarily—and then went to the living room to plan how I intended to be discovered.

I looked at the small bakelite desk clock which stood on my writing desk. I probably had another ten or fifteen minutes before I could expect Crennan. So much had changed since I first came to the house. My return to the crawl space under the house reminded me of how my condition had altered since I had first discovered the (almost) empty house.

In those days, I was in the thick of my living as an urban homesteader. Indeed, I still have all my notes for my book on the topic: Urban Homesteading—Surviving in the Urban Wild, to which I hope to return when my current set of projects is complete. The only tenet of urban homesteading is to live 'in the wild' of the urban environment as if it were any other wild environment. In the yet to be written book, I present urban homesteading as a life-choice, which it may be for some. It wasn't, of course, for me. 'Urban Homesteading' just sounds better than 'homeless'.

I had happened upon Norma's house in my random peregrinations. Urban homesteaders do a lot of walking around. It looked promising. The garden was unkempt. The house was shabby, but not derelict. The street was quiet, suburban, prosperous. Tick, tick, tick. It was late autumn and identifying secure, dry sleeping spaces was an everyday necessity. I noted the address and resolved to return in the evening to check for lights.

That evening, I returned with the small backpack I called home to find there were no lights on. I walked into the front garden, carefully shutting the gate behind me while checking to see if any neighbours were watching me. No one was. I walked through the long grass of the front yard and through to the side of the house, listening for any sounds of activity, looking for any means of gaining access to a dry spot to spend the night. That's when I found the small gate which led to the crawl space under the house. The bolt was stiff but easily opened. There was still enough light for me to make my way under the house and crawl forward to find the roll of carpet and underfelt. For an urban homesteader, this was like a business traveller finding that the single, standard room he had booked had been

The best form of defence

upgraded to the Presidential Suite. I unrolled enough of the carpet to provide me with a warm sleeping spot. I took off my shoes, unrolled the nylon quilt from around the backpack and settled down for the night, still listening for any sounds of life in the house above.

I woke in the early morning to the comforting sound of light, Melbourne rain: steady, soaking rain. It was comforting because I was warm and dry. I had heard nothing in the house above me in the night, apart from the usual animal scratchings of possums or rats. As I lay in the warmth of my carpet and quilt cocoon, I listened for any sounds of a household waking up. There was nothing. I resolved to doze for as long as my bladder would let me and then to explore the backyard of the house. I was certain by now that the house was empty. Although my crib under the house was comfortable enough, I was hoping there might be a shed or even an outdoor toilet in the backyard which I could use as needed in the coming winter months.

When I finally crept out from under the house, it was still raining, which suited me because it reduced the risk of neighbours seeing me and asking awkward questions. The yard behind the house was more overgrown than the front. On one side of the yard was a small garden shed — a classic sixties fibro garden shed with a small window, rusting corrugated iron roof, and a tongue and groove door — which was locked with an old padlock. The security arrangements wouldn't have slowed a determined child, but a glance through the window showed there was nothing inside likely to be of any value.[5]

In the rear corner of the yard, on the opposite side of the shed, was a small brick garage. The door leading from the garden into the garage was not locked. Inside was Betsy, the perfectly

---

[5] I later learnt how wrong I had been. Clearing out the shed revealed a pristine Victa 18" Rotomo in immaculate condition. The original operating manual was preserved in the drawer of an small desk used as a potting table, only slightly chawed by silverfish.

The best form of defence

preserved Toyota Tiara, dusty, but still looking as though she was in serviceable condition. I could see the folding doors which opened to allow access to the lane behind the property were locked with a solid bar of hardwood. As a potential campsite, the garage was too small with Betsy in it to interest me and the shed looked even less promising. I shut the door of the garage and, after relieving myself in an overgrown elder bush, I turned back, intending to return under the house and wait for the rain to cease.

The house was clearly unoccupied and I thought that in a house of this age there might be an outside laundry or toilet which might prove useful. One of the most difficult problems confronting the urban homesteader is the finding and securing of safe places to store temporarily the meagre possessions one has foraged. I walked up to the small back verandah. There was no outside laundry. I opened the flywire screen door and tried the back door. It was locked, but it was only a single latch key lock. I peered through the keyhole and saw that the key was in the lock. I wasn't yet committed to the idea of looking inside the house, but it was handy to know I wouldn't have any trouble if I wanted to. I returned to my crib under the house, wrapped myself in my quilt, and went to sleep listening to the rain and a blackbird happily scratching around in the wilds of the garden.

My reminiscences of my first coming to the house were interrupted by a sound at the side of the house.

This was no blackbird.

I felt my stomach tighten and my bowels loosen.

I listened intently and thought I could make out Crennan's progress to the back of the house. I was sitting at the desk. I had a notepad and pen in front of me. My hands were shaking too much to trust myself to be writing anything; so I flicked a couple of pages back in the notepad so I could pretend to be reading my notes. There was a framed picture of a seaside on the wall in front of the desk. In the reflection of the glass, I could see the door to the living room; so I would know when he was behind me.

Crennan was so cautious in his approach that I began to wonder if I'd imagined the noise. Perhaps he hadn't seen me leave his house? Perhaps I was going to spend a long night of anxiety for no reason.

The back door opened slowly. I heard the door lock being released carefully. I heard the fly wire door being very gently shut behind it. Crennan was inside the house.

I watched the second hand of the bakelite clock swing slowly around the dial. I watched it make a second complete rotation. Crennan wasn't going to be rushed.

"Get on with it, Crennan!" I called.

I abandoned the pretence of reading the notepad while watching the reflection in the picture. I was never going to be able to pull it off. My hands were shaking too much.

Still, he took his time. I turned in the chair to face the doorway, but there was nothing.

"If you're worried about a trap, or something, don't," I called to him. "I don't need any help dealing with a turd like you."

That brought him along the corridor, but still he waited to one side of the door. Although I was expecting him, I still jumped when he leaped into the doorway, crouching and waving his handgun in front of him.

"Jesus!" I exclaimed. "You scared me. Very CSI. Very profesh, Crennan."

He was still pointing the handgun at me.

"Shut up." His eyes darted around the room, still wary of walking into a trap.

"I've told you, there's no trap. I haven't rigged a net to fall on you."

"Shut the fuck up," he spat the words at me. "Where is she?"

The best form of defence

"Put the gun down, Crennan. You're not going to shoot me with your service pistol."

I hoped to hell it was his service pistol. It was. I saw him hesitate, but he kept it pointed at me. I thought it best to press home whatever advantage I could.

"Put the gun down, Crennan. And are you wondering, Senior Constable Crennan, why I keep using your name loudly?"

He didn't answer.

"Because, Crennan, you won't find the recording of your visit, but I imagine the homicide squad will be better resourced. So put the gun away and say what you have to say."

I don't know if he bought the idea that I might be recording the visit, but he slipped the gun inside his shirt where I assumed he was concealing the holster.

He took a step into the room, still flicking his eyes from side to side.

"Where is she, shithead?"

"Well, not here, obviously."

He stepped closer to me. He could see I was scared. It pleased him. He came closer, only stopping when he was directly in front of me, looking down at me. He bent down so that his face was almost touching mine.

"Last time," he breathed softly. "Where is she?"

"Wow, regulation hard man stuff."

It might have been more impressive if my voice had been steady. Crennan pulled me forward off the chair and slung me to the ground. He dropped his knee into my stomach and gripped me around the throat with his right hand.

Allow me to break the narrative here for a moment to describe the pain and fear. When he landed on his knee on my stomach (or solar plexus, I suppose Dr No would have been able to tell me) I felt a simultaneous explosion of pain and nausea. I tried to gasp for air but couldn't breathe. His hand around my throat wasn't helping, but something else was preventing me from breathing. As I stared at the rabid fury on his face, the great wave of pain receded and left the sea-wrack of panic. I knew I was going to die. I gasped and gulped, a fish on the sand. I started thrashing about in panic, incapable of rational thought. I was saved by Crennan and his disgust for my weakness. He pushed himself upright, thrusting with unnecessary force on my throat. I rolled over to my side, still gasping for air.

"One last time…" — naturally, he couldn't leave the hard man clichés after he'd worked so hard at them — "where is she?"

Crennan, doubtless, had his share of pleasure in life. There were moments I am sure which he regarded as wonderful, moments when he felt he had surpassed himself, transcended his limitations, but I was about to experience something Crennan could never even imagine: inspiration. When genius asserts itself, one must simply accept and respond. I knew what to do. I shat myself.

Curled on one side, still gasping, but at least now getting some air into my lungs, I burbled unintelligible syllables while I emptied my bowels into the welcoming expanse of my underpants. The smell assaulted the Crennan nose.

"Jesus! You fat fuck!"

I remember wondering if fear could make one's shit smell worse. It certainly seemed to.

"I'll take you." I was still gasping for breath.

"What?"

"I'll take you to her."

Crennan could hardly bear to be in the same room.

"Just tell me where she is, arsehole."

"I'll have to drive you. I dropped her off at a house she knew. Don't know the address."

"But you can find it again?"

I nodded as I lay there curled in a stinking croissant of defeat.

"Get up," he commanded, "and clean yourself up."

I rose cautiously to my feet, as I stood, the bolus of shit in my underpants felt reassuringly heavy.

"Bathroom..." I pointed.

"Get moving. Jesus you stink!"

Crennan indicated for me to lead. He followed as closely behind as his olfactory revulsion allowed.

"Leave the door open!" he insisted as I opened the door to the toilet.

He stood close to the door, enjoying my humiliation as I stepped clumsily out of my shoes, dropped my trousers and set them aside, and then inched the underpants down my legs and stepped out, first one leg, then the second. I stood, still holding the—this should have been a clue, Senior Constable!—still holding the underpants like David's sling.

Crennan smirked at me: naked from the waist down, snail trails of shit down one leg, holding a small sack of my own shit. I let me enjoy his moment watching me, assuming my humiliation. I let him raise his eyes, sneering as his eyes wiped over my genitals, and then look directly in my face. I watched his contempt change to puzzlement as he saw me smiling at him.

"Oh, Crennan, who's locked and loaded now?"

I flung the stinking bola into his face and as he turned involuntarily to avoid it, a small cry of disgust escaping like gas, I threw myself onto him. The underpants connected with the side of his head and even as I launched myself at him, he was trying to wipe the shit off his face, scrabbling at it as if he'd walked into a spider's web. The weight of my impact knocked him down and I fell on top of him. My underpants were lying next to us. I grabbed them and rubbed them into his face, eyes and nose. His first instinct was to protect his face with his hands and then push me away, leaving me to jump to my feet and fall on him again before he'd had time to move, driving both knees into his chest. He let out a moan of pain.

The best form of defence

I am not an imaginative fighter. I apologise for the tediousness of the description, but if I am to remain true to the events of that night, a little repetition is called for. Quite a lot, actually.

I jumped to my feet again and repeated the procedure. Crennan tried to roll out of my way, but my own fear of what might happen should he regain his feet propelled me. I was a maddened elephant stomping a lion. I jumped up, I drove my knees into him. Something cracked. I jumped up, I drove my knees into him. More cracking, a sharp cry of pain, and more moaning. I jumped up, I drove my knees into him. He had curled himself into a ball to try to save his ribs and chest. I was tiring, so I began to focus on his head and neck. The first time one of my knees landed on his temple, his body gave an electric jolt. I thought of Luigi Galvani and his string of dead frogs' legs. By the third or fourth time my knees landed on his neck and the side of his head, I realised that the movements I was detecting in Crennan were only the equal and opposite reaction of my body landing on his. Luigi's battery was flat. I stamped on his neck a couple of times for good measure, but neither I nor Sabasa had anything more to fear from Crennan. Crennan had left the world nothing more than a long mess for me to clean up.

*

The superfluity of men

Extract from the unpublished work, 'Masculinear', by Thomas Furphy

Biologically, the male is largely superfluous. If all the human males on the planet were to die immediately, the species would not be threatened (unless it were from diseases spread by all the decomposing bodies, but let us suppose that, along with all simultaneously dying, all trace of them disappeared into the ether). The species would not be threatened. There are always enough pregnant women waddling around to ensure that, after a break of fifteen years or so, the species would get back to pumping out babies.

If all the human females disappeared, however, the species would be defunct. Perhaps advances in in vitro reproductive techniques might

The best form of defence

help, but I doubt it. Males are largely superfluous; women are essential.

You can imagine (one might say, dream) of a world in which there were so few men that they travelled around the country in jolly bands, setting up shop in whatever town they came to, offering to service the women of the town for a fortnight or so before packing up and moving to the next town.

In the happy world envisaged in the previous paragraph, it is unlikely that there would ever be wars. As long as there were few enough men, all happily marching from town to town and all satisfactorily shagged out at the end of each day, it is hard to imagine anyone needing to take up arms about anything. If we ever get to the stage of being able to engineer our DNA in a sophisticated enough way, I would recommend that the ratio of female to male offspring produced should be about 1000:1.

I know there will be those who cry out that reducing the number of males produced will mean we miss out on all that male vigour, spirit, imagination, genius. But would we? The world's population now is at least a thousand times bigger than the population of England until the late eighteenth century. A population of that size produced Chaucer, Sir Francis Drake, Shakespeare, Newton, James Cook and a thousand other worthy chaps. We would still have the capacity to produce those sort of fellows; we'd just be missing all the poor mugs who serve in the ranks.

Patently, most of the planet's problems are caused by too many males infesting the place. If we leave speculation and concentrate on the now, the challenge for men living in our current, imperfectly gender-balanced world, is 'what to do about it?' How should men confront the problem of this superfluity of men?

© Copyright 2016, Thom Furphy

*

A little spot of housework; a little bit of history

> Removed the rubbish in the hall, but still have to arrange to have the old carpet and underfelt removed. Began design and construction of the dual bin composting system—leaving concrete base to dry and will try rolling compost bins before bothering to complete a more robust solution...

The moments after Crennan's demotion from sentient being and bacterial host to simple bacterial host are hard for me to remember. The notes in my journal, written the following morning, aren't much help. I do remember starting to shake. I think the first thing I did was pick up my underpants, carry them to the kitchen, wrap them in a plastic bag, and throw them in the bin. Then I walked back down the hall and stood looking at Crennan's body. It wasn't Crennan's anymore. It was my body now. Finders keepers.

I was unsure when rigor mortis would set in and I puzzled about the best position in which to arrange him to allow for the easiest disposal of the body if I needed to do it once his muscles were locked. I wondered about arranging him in a circle, head to knees; that would allow me to bury him in a compact, circular hole which would be easy to disguise as a flower bed. I wanted to avoid any new rectangular flower beds suddenly appearing in the garden. But I rejected the idea. I didn't want to plant any flowers above that bastard.

I walked around the body and grasped his ankles and pulled him straight, pushing the body against the skirting board so I would be able to walk past him easily. I knew I would have to get him out of the house before I could thoroughly clean the corridor, but I was feeling too weak. I arranged his arms to lie along his side, and then I walked past him to the bathroom and had one of the top three most necessary showers of my life.

A little spot of housework; a little bit of history

As I stood under the shower, letting the warm water wash away the shit, tension, fear, and horror of the past hour, I tried to turn my mind to the pressing problem of what-the-hell-to-do-next. The most pressing problem, of course, was about six foot long and stretched out in my hall. My next most pressing... I realised that compared to the hallway problem, there was nothing else worth thinking about; so I thought about the hallway problem.

I could not resolve it tonight. Disposing of a body, as I knew only too well, is not easy, but if I couldn't resolve all the details of the disposal, I had to be on the way to resolving them. One detail I had to have decided, was how to conceal the corpse from immediate, accidental discovery. That would give me time to decide on a hiding place that would conceal Crennan from any future, more systematic and thorough search.

Relatively quickly[6], I had a plan to conceal the body—a plan which eliminated the difficulty of transporting the body, but which respected my sincere desire to afford Crennan no courtesy or respect. But even as I congratulated myself on having a plan, I realised that a greater problem than the disposal of Crennan the Body was the disposal of Crennan the Person. I had two clear objectives: I needed to be able to convince Sabasa that Crennan was no threat and would never appear to threaten her again (without, obviously, telling her that he'd played jumping castle to my inner six year old's birthday party); and I needed to eliminate, or minimise, the efforts Crennan's ex-colleagues took to find their pal. It was as the water played over my hair and down my face and neck that the necessity for the haircut became apparent.

---

[6] I'm not sure what I'm measuring my speed of resolution against. Perhaps most murderers who haven't had time to plan their activities resolve the problem of corpse disposal without the need for a twenty minute shower. Perhaps I should have said 'Relatively slowly'. I don't really know, relatively or otherwise.

Crennan and I were not dissimilar. He was at least a decade younger than I, but we were about the same height, and, despite Crennan's referring to me as a 'fat fuck', I was not much heavier. True, my weight was slightly differently arranged, and my belt was a hole or two longer than his, but I realised in the shower that I could make a reasonable Crennan as long as I kept my intellect hidden. The main, external difference between us was that I kept my hair sensibly cut while Crennan affected an appalling man/boy haircut with a central cowlick of hair gelled like a tiny dorsal fin upright on his head[7]. His haircut was all the more dreadful for being half-hearted. I presume police regulations prevented him from anything more extreme.

If I had my hair cut to resemble Crennan's, I could make a reasonable stab at passing for Crennan. Naturally, I could never pass for him in front of anyone who knew him, but I would be able to pass myself off as Crennan well enough for people who didn't know him to think they had seen Crennan should they be asked a week later. My plan, still forming in my mind, was to call in sick to his station and then, posing as Crennan, find a suitably harassed medico to diagnose me with depression and write me a medical certificate for a few days leave. I would try to extend the sick leave for as long as possible, and at the end of the sick leave, I would email my resignation, citing my depression as the reason and then Crennan would be heard of no more. Should any of his colleagues investigate, all they would find was an empty house.

I got out of the shower and began drying myself. I would work out the details later. I had the bones of the plan to eliminate

---

[7] I believe this hairstyle is called a 'faux-hawk', but I may be mistaken. Not as criminally mistaken as any man who affects the haircut, mind you.

Crennan the person. Now I turned my attention to problem of disposing of Crennan the cadaver.

Luckily, I had had to resolve a similar problem once before; so much of the preliminary thinking had already been done. In the first days of my living at Norma's, I had lived under the house. It was two or three days before I decided to break in to see if there was anything inside worth foraging. This was taking the idea of urban homesteading to its most extreme. Perhaps it was taking it beyond its most extreme and squarely into criminality. Nonetheless, I was motivated more by curiosity than avarice. Although I knew by then the house was empty, I expected an owner to turn up eventually, and I was sure that anything of monetary value would have been taken out of the house, but there might still be things of real use to me, even if they were no use to anyone else: a saucepan, a blanket, a cushion or pillow. Who knew what treasure might lie within?

The back door of Norma's house was solid, but only locked with a latch key left in the lock. There are several ways past a latch key lock. The simplest involves stout boots and a couple of well-directed kicks. This method is loud and damages the door. A second method, much in vogue in early sixties television shows, has the would-be burglar slide a piece of newspaper under the door, push the key out of the lock and onto the paper, and then neatly withdraw the newspaper with the key still lying on it. Unfortunately, the builders of Norma's house had built the doorway with a strip of hardwood on the outside of the lower edge of the door, protecting the house from the twin dangers of sixties television fans and draughts. I resorted to a third method, knowing I could always resort to method one if it failed. I fashioned a small length of old coat hanger wire into an L-shaped hook, and, with a fair amount of jiggling, was able to flick the key around in the lock and open the door without damaging either the door or the lock.

I stepped inside Norma's house cautiously. I knew there was no one inside, because I'd lived underneath it long enough, but, of course, I was wrong. The house was musty and had a rich smell, which I first thought was the result of possum infestation, but after creeping through the kitchen and back rooms, I found the cause of the smell in Norma's bedroom: Norma. She had died on her bed and was still cocooned in her flannelette sheets, Onkaparinga blankets, and paisley covered eiderdown. You might think the smell was dreadful, but she must have been dead for some time. The room smelt musty and sweet, with notes of damp carpet, but wasn't unbearable. It was strangely peaceful. I walked quietly through the rest of the house, not disturbing anything, feeling as though I had entered a tomb and felt honoured to be allowed to witness the house in which this woman had lived, untouched since the night of her death.

I returned briefly to Norma's room to bid her goodnight, and then left again through the back door, keeping the key with me to lock it from the outside. I slept that night again under the house while I considered what I should do.

The plan to inhabit the house grew organically. I could be fairly sure from the state of the house and the fact of Norma's undiscovered body that Norma didn't have any close friends or family looking in on her. Perhaps she had none at all. I resolved to investigate the house more thoroughly in the morning, looking, in particular, for documents to explain who owned the house, who might come looking around for it, anything to help me make a reasonable case for staying in the house for a few weeks, or, if lucky, a month or two. I never expected that I might soon be planning to own the property.

In the morning, I re-entered the house and began my examination. Now that it was light outside, I could risk turning on a light to see if the electricity was still connected. It was. Water and gas were also still connected. This was slightly puzzling, but it would mean I could cook a hot meal if I wanted. In those days, the prospect of a warm meal was the height of my ambitions. I examined the house carefully, avoiding Norma's room for the time being. In the front hall, pushed under the door were dozens of window-faced envelopes—presumably the electricity, gas, and water bills. I had seen a letterbox at the front of the property; so it seemed that someone was emptying the letterbox for her and pushing the letters under the door. The postie? Possibly. A neighbour? More likely.

I collected the pile of envelopes and took them through to the living room where I'd seen a small desk. I drew back the curtains to let some light into the room and began a forensic examination of Norma's affairs. It was ridiculously easy. Norma was a brilliantly organised woman. She had a simple but effective filing system for all her bills, statements, and correspondence: each quarter's notices were collected together, a small square of notepaper labelled with the year and quarter was folded around the papers, and the pile was fastened with a clothes peg. These were then neatly stacked in a cardboard box under the desk. The box under the desk contained several years of filing, and I would later discover that Norma kept seven years of filing in boxes in a cupboard in the living room, but the treasure trove of correspondence allowed me to know where she banked, what her bank account contained, which shares she had and the dividends received, which utility companies she used, and so on. Norma had arranged almost all her utility bills to be automatically paid from her bank account. The pile of letters by the front door weren't bills; they were statements. If I hadn't stumbled into the house, her estate would have been quietly eaten up by her service providers. I was also able to surmise, from the dates on the earliest letters in the hallway, the approximate date of her death: she might have been dead for approximately eighteen months. I also learnt her name, of course: Norma Selfe.

A little spot of housework; a little bit of history

As I sat there, marvelling at how self-possessed, how organised and efficient Norma had been, I realised that there was nothing to stop me keeping the household running. Norma had money in the bank and a small but regular income from shares. If Norma could live on her modest income, I, a master of urban homesteading and living on nothing, could do very nicely on it.

The next few days were spent cleaning myself up, getting to know Norma and her household well, and planning my extended residence. I kept the door to Norma's room shut when I wasn't examining the possessions she kept there, but I found her presence strangely comforting. I took to wishing her good morning and good night—not in a crude, jesting way, but with respect that grew to a genuine fondness for her. I introduced myself to her neighbours on either side as a nephew who had come to help her maintain her independence. I explained her absence by telling them that she had gone into respite care at an aged care facility, but that was expected to be only a short-term arrangement and the family wanted her to be back living in her own home as soon as possible.

I discovered that Barry, her neighbour on the east side, had been responsible for walking her letters from the letterbox and pushing them under the door. He'd been on the verge of calling the police to check on her, but because the property was still being maintained (Norma had a gardening service she paid— too much, in my opinion—which mowed the lawns every four to six weeks), he assumed all was in order. I suspect that Barry was keeping an eye on the property with a view to buying it at a knockdown rate, but I may be doing him a disservice. I have certainly found Barry to be an excellent neighbour and a fund of knowledge about all things mechanical, electrical, and automotive.

And so, with the ease of an eel moving through pond weed, I found myself installed, Norma's nephew Thom, as her carer. I found Norma's spidery signature on several documents and

A little spot of housework; a little bit of history

was soon able to reproduce it well enough to have myself added as a signatory to her accounts at her bank. Everyone was extremely helpful to me and all wished Norma a speedy return from respite care. She had clearly been a bit of a favourite with all who knew her. In all Norma's documents, I could find no reference to any solicitors; so I was unable to determine if she had deposited a will with anyone. I certainly could find no will in the house and so was unable to tell if she had relatives or others with a better claim to her estate than I. I could also find no letters or other personal communications from anyone in the past decade. The last letter she had kept was from someone called Clarrie Fong. It was a short letter describing not much, written in a shaky hand from an address in rural New South Wales. This led me to conclude that Norma was one of life's true orphans and, as a fellow orphan, I was as close to family as she had. I visited a local solicitor, explained the situation to him, and for a very moderate fee, I was able to have him draw up a deed conferring enduring power of attorney for Norma Selfe to me, and, once I had taken it back to the aged care home and had her sign it, witnessed by an illegible nursing aide, I had control of Norma's estate.

*

Why should we need lawyers?

Extract from A Programme of Moderate Political Reform in Australia, www.pmpra.com

Just as it once made sense that a largely illiterate population should elect a small number of citizens to represent them in parliament, it once made sense that a small number of educated and literate professionals should make their living advising and assisting citizens in legal matters. Does it still make sense?

In our present society, we need lawyers. We need them to draw up wills, to assist in the conveyancing of property, to advise and advocate when marriages break down, to defend us if we are accused of crime. Why do we need them? We need them because no one who has not been thoroughly schooled in the arcane practice of the law can possibly manage those tasks simply by reading the law.

This is wrong. Worse, it is not necessary.

The reason you cannot read the laws pertaining to, say, transfer of property and be confident that you can now act lawfully and in your own interests in conducting the purchase or sale of land is because the laws are written in a way which is deliberately, shamefully, obfuscatory.

How can we improve the situation? We can rewrite our laws in plain English. We can determine that all laws should be able to be understood by any citizen of normal intelligence and rewrite them accordingly. If it is not reasonable for citizens to represent themselves in most situations in our courts, the problem is not with the citizens, but with the legal system itself and we need to change it.

It might be argued that rewriting our laws is so massive a job, that it is impractical. It is not impractical; it is a big job. It will need time and resources. We can find time and resources to host Olympic Games, to go on military adventures overseas, to build freeways, to fund the bread and circuses beloved of modern democracies; why shouldn't we fund the reorganisation and rewriting of our laws? It may take ten years. It may take twenty. It's worth it. And it gives the great army of solicitors and barristers time enough to retrain as something useful.

*

As I came to be more and more solidly established in my new home, I realised that I could not leave Norma in her bed any longer, but I had grown fond of her and I wanted to provide her with a suitable final resting place. I hit upon the idea of burying her in her own backyard—it seemed the place that had meant most to her—but I wanted to provide her with a suitable memorial, one that I hoped she might have approved of and one which honoured her and her home. The front garden contained a row of neglected rose bushes, and I thought of creating a rose garden in the front of the house, but the practical requirement of privacy while burying a body eliminated using the front garden. In Norma's bedroom was a framed, Japanese print of goldfish swimming in a pond, gentle fronds of water plants framing their paths. This gave me the idea of creating an ornamental pond in the backyard, one I would stock with goldfish and water plants, for Norma to rest beneath. In order to ensure that no one found it odd that I should start excavating the backyard, I approached Barry for his advice.

"Barry, I'm going to be doing a bit of tidying up around the house while Norma's in respite care. There's some joinery repairs in the kitchen and damp in the bathroom. I'll need to get her a new mattress, too. But I was looking at the backyard and thinking it looked pretty bleak. I thought it might be nice for her to come home to an ornamental pond—she's always loved goldfish. Somewhere we could sit in the afternoons and she could feed the fish. What do you think?"

Barry made a non-committal grunt, suspicious that I might be about to ask him to contribute to digging it, perhaps.

"Thing is, I don't know a lot about how to do it. I've looked up fibreglass ponds, which look all right, but do you just dig a hole and plonk them in?"

Barry sprang to life. "No, no, you'd want to bed the pond in sand, builders' sand, at least, and preferably on top of a layer of crushed rock. If I were you, I'd dig a hole at least six inches deeper than the depth of the pond. I'd fill at least three inches with screenings, crushed bluemetal maybe, and then three inches of sand. I pound that flat—and get it *absolutely* level— and then you could bed the pond on that. That'll be stable and ensure you don't have any rocks or other things that might rupture the fibreglass skin. Water's heavy, you know."

"Beauty, thanks, Barry."

"Do you want a hand?" he asked weakly.

A little spot of housework; a little bit of history

I pretended to consider the offer.

"No, thanks for the offer, but I'd really like to do this myself for Norma. I might come over occasionally to ask your advice, if you don't mind?"

"Happy to help!"

That afternoon, I went off to a garden supply depot, found a five foot, half-round pond which would more than cover Norma's tiny frame, curled as it was into a neat semi-circle, and began marking out the pond's future location.

I had Barry's advice to thank for the excuse to dig a hole far deeper than the depth of the pond. I ordered the screenings and the sand for the next day and prepared the hole for the pond. I dug it at least two feet deeper than required and loosened the soil below that. That night I continued to dig out the pond hole until it was three to four feet deeper than required. I swaddled Norma in her paisley quilt, wrapped the whole, tiny bundle in the woollen rug she had by her bed, and carried her out to the garden and laid her gently in the hole. It was like carrying a bird. I had found an old, hand-knitted scarf in Richmond colours in a drawer with a signed photograph of Jack Dyer and a football record of a match between Richmond and North Melbourne. I placed those treasures, along with a threadbare, knitted teddy bear, in the grave with her. I then covered her body with two foot of soil, tamped the base flat and left the hole ready to receive the screenings, sand, and pond.

In the morning, when the screening and sand were delivered, I followed Barry's advice and raked a layer of three inches of screenings and covered it with the same depth of sand. I moved the pond into position and adjusted the sand layer until the pond was perfectly level and its edge was sitting about half an inch proud of the lawn. Barry had advised me that, with the weight of the water, the pond would settle down over the next few months. I filled the pond with water and then went next door to invite Barry to see the results of my work and his advice.

"Very nice," Barry nodded his approval. "Now, where are you going to run the electricity?"

"Electricity?"

"You'll want a pump and a fountain, won't you? To keep the water aerated?"

"Hadn't thought of it."

"It'll get very smelly very quickly otherwise."

Odd smells in the backyard were something I wanted to avoid, but I certainly didn't want an electrician digging a trench to run a cable along; so that afternoon, I revisited the hardware shop and invested in a solar powered pump and fountain, some water plants, and some bulbs to plant around the perimeter of the pond. It was a fulfilling project. I was motivated by the practical need to have a secure resting place for Norma, but the more effort I put into making it beautiful for her, the happier and more contented I became. By the time I had stocked the pond with half a dozen goldfish and a variety of pond plants, I felt warmly sure that Norma would have approved of her memorial.

So, all in all, the burial of Norma was a satisfying and pleasant job, but one of the chief reasons it had been pleasant was that I'd had plenty of time. The disposal of Crennan's body was quite different. Norma was tiny and her bird-like frame had been desiccated over time. Crennan was above average height, well-muscled, and still full of most of his bodily fluids. Norma had died a natural death and I could not possibly be implicated. Crennan had my footprints all over him. I needed to dispose of Crennan quickly, before he began decomposing too noticeably, and I needed to dispose of him in a way that would render his discovery unlikely.

After my long shower, I dressed and turned my attention to disposing of Crennan. I was exhausted. I knew that I needed to sleep before I tackled anything too demanding. At the same time, I needed to conceal his body in the interim. I took a torch, went outside, and crawled under the house. I left the computer tucked up in its roll of carpet, but retrieved the roll of underfelt. I dragged it into the hall and unrolled a couple of metres of it. I then dragged Crennan's body onto the underfelt, rolled it over him, and then dragged the whole bundle out the back door and left him cocooned in underfelt on the back verandah. I reasoned that the underfelt would be absorbent enough to trap any leakage from Crennan's body and any uncertain odours could be attributed to damp underfelt.

I locked the back door, washed my hands, and went to bed. I slept for nine hours, dreamlessly, deeply asleep.

I awoke next morning feeling refreshed, but sore. The muscles in my arms and legs were stiff; I had strained my lower back and my right knee was bruised and sore where I had landed on the gun Crennan had concealed in his shirt. I breakfasted slowly, gingerly moving about the kitchen, realising I needed to work this day to ensure I could permanently dispose of Crennan. I briefly pondered the possibility of buying a wood chipper and spreading Crennan as mulch around the garden, but, pleasing as this might have been aesthetically, I doubted that the domestic wood chipper could deal with an adult male thigh bone. The wood chipper did lead me to the ultimate solution, however.

As I ate my porridge and sipped my way through a light Oolong tea, I browsed through Norma's copy of The Australian

Gardener[8]. I was looking for plans for a traditional, double box composting bin. And there it was. Recommended dimensions of each compartment: 3 foot by 3 foot. Just about perfect for covering a six foot cadaver. I mightn't be able to shred Crennan and feed him to the worms, but I could do the next best thing and bury him underneath the compost. Every time I salted it with manure, I'd think of him.

That morning, I popped over to see Barry with my Brunnings, ostensibly to get his advice on timber for the frame of the compost bins, but really just to alert him to my planned activities next to the boundary fence. I would place the compost bins in the far corner of the backyard as close to the boundary fence as practical. It was a dark corner, unlikely to be disturbed anytime in the future, particularly if it was covered in composting bins, but I wanted to make sure Barry wouldn't be too inquisitive about my roiling around there. Barry was not enthusiastic.

"Double bin composting? Why bother, mate? Get one of those rotating drums—much more efficient. Neater looking, too."

"I was thinking something more traditional would suit the place better..." I countered feebly.

"No way! Too much bloody work, son. They used to make compost that way, but it's too bloody hard. And too much to go wrong. If you don't turn the compost over, you risk it going sour—and it *stinks* if it's sour. It'll take you six months to fill the bin with compost, and then you've got to try to shovel it out from the bottom because the stuff on the bottom always rots down first. No. Take my tip: get a rotating composting drum. I've got one. It's a dream."

---

[8] 1924 20th Edition, blue cloth cover with a full colour plate of an Australian home set in an English garden by Leslie H. Brunning.

I retreated from the contest. If I persevered with my double compartment composting bin, Barry would take altogether too much interest in it, watching for opportunities to tell me he'd been right. I wanted Barry to believe that whatever I did in that corner of the garden had been his idea. I returned to Barry later that morning with a new plan.

"Been thinking about the composting, and I'm sure you're right. No way I'm going to be turning compost over with a fork. So I thought what I'd do is clear a space in that back corner, and get a couple of those composting drums as you recommended: one to be filling while the other is composting."

"Yep. That'd work okay. You need to rotate the drums a couple of times a week."

"That shouldn't be a problem." I paused and then added, "And perhaps I should pave a few feet—a little concrete patch—to sit the drums on so it's not too muddy underfoot."

Barry nodded appreciatively. He was a big fan of concrete. "Let me know if you want to borrow the mixer."

So I retained the original dimensions of the two compartment compost bin and started dig out the hole for the concrete. The ground was difficult to dig, compacted and thick with shrub roots. I headed over to Barry's to borrow his steel wrecking bar to loosen the ground. I couldn't avoid Barry offering to bring it over and take a look. I did my best to dissuade him—I had an awkward roll of underfelt on my back verandah that I wasn't keen on anyone investigating—but Barry wasn't to be denied his opportunity to advise.

"You're clearing a pretty big patch for a couple of compost bins," he started unsurely.

A little spot of housework; a little bit of history

"Well, I thought if ever I did get enthusiastic enough I might one day make the double bins."

"Fair enough. Your funeral!" he chuckled, incorrectly. "You won't need much depth for a small slab," he continued, thrusting the wrecking bar into the soil and levering up a small clod, "but you'll need to go down a foot or so. Biggest mistake people make is not giving themselves enough depth."

It wasn't a mistake I was going to make.

"Anyway, I'll leave you to it," said Barry as he passed the wrecking bar to me. "Just leave it around the back when you're finished. Don't bother washing it down or anything," he added, clearly meaning that I should wash it down before returning it. He started walking back towards the side gate when the roll of underfelt on my verandah began ringing.

Barry stopped and turned to me, puzzled. "Your phone?"

I thrust the wrecking bar into the soil and hurried over to the back door.

"Yes, left it inside. Thanks for your help, Barry."

Barry turned with a wave and headed off down the side of the house. As soon as I heard the click of the side gate and knew Barry was headed home, I started scrabbling at the roll of underfelt, lifting up one edge, trying to unroll it enough to get to Crennan's phone. In the haste of my panic, I lifted the edge of the roll too quickly, too vigorously, unrolling Crennan too close to the edge of the verandah: he rolled off and lay in an expanding line of brown underfelt as the rest of the roll gracefully unfurled across the garden.

A little spot of housework; a little bit of history

I stood, stupefied on the verandah, holding an edge of stinking underfelt. The phone in Crennan's pocket now sounded like a klaxon, shrieking to the world of the horror I had committed.

I came to my senses and threw my end of the underfelt over Crennan and began rolling him back into the underfelt, sausage meat into a pastry sheet. The phone continued ringing, thankfully now muffled again. I sat on the roll and waited for it to stop, looking around me, terrified that someone had witnessed Crennan's final exhibition of bastardry.

No one had. The phone stopped.

Rather than lug Crennan back onto the verandah, I dragged him over to the corner where I was digging and wrestled the roll of underfelt half under the bushes while I continued to dig out the compost pit. It was exhausting work. I had to use Barry's wrecking bar to loosen the soil by six inches or so, then shovel it out to one side and begin again with the wrecking bar. I had been working for an hour or so when the underfelt began ringing again. I listened for any sound on Barry's side of the fence, but he wasn't around. I let the phone ring out again, but knew I'd have to retrieve it before it rang again.

My arms were aching, but I couldn't rest. I dragged the Crennan sausage roll out from under the bushes and began a careful, forensic peeling away of the underfelt until I had the body exposed, but with a large tongue of underfelt ready to throw over him should the need arise.

I was surprised how dead he looked.

He no longer looked like an unconscious body. He looked dead. Norma never looked dead. She looked a little walnutty, in need of a really good moisturiser, but she didn't look like a cadaver. Crennan looked grey and cold and dead.

A little spot of housework; a little bit of history

I began the distasteful task of going through all his pockets. I assembled a small pile of possessions next to the body: wallet, coins, the phone, house keys, car keys, pens. Then I fished out his service pistol from under his shirt. It had come out of the holster in our tussle. I left him his empty holster. That's symbolism, that is. I scooped all his personal detritus together, threw the flap of underfelt over the body, taking the booty inside for later inspection. I returned to the backyard, rolled the body, loosely swaddled in underfelt, back under the shrubs. I didn't bother trying to re-package him too carefully because I wanted him under soil as soon as possible.

I returned to my wrecking bar and shovel. I was tempted to knock off and have a cup of tea, but I kept at the task at hand, arms and back aching, my knee throbbing. Crennan's phone rang inside the house twice more before midday, by which time I had a pit deep enough to accommodate him.

I looked around me, checking no one (living) had suddenly materialised in the yard, dragged Crennan over to the side of the hole and rolled him in. He landed on his face, one arm beneath him, one arm crooked behind his back, frozen in preparation for a formal bow, or caught in the moment before he was to skip into a complex set of steps for a minuet. He looked like the prat he was. I shovelled dirt on top of him and filled the pit to within a foot of the top. I took some pleasure in tamping it down thoroughly. Stomping methodically over the entire site to make it secure and level.

"Try rolling out of that, you prick," was his eulogy.

More housework; more history

> ... Spent an unpleasant hour today cleaning up the mess in the hall. The smell of my faeces is alarming. I must remember to have a bowel cancer check up with Dr N. Will need to give myself a new haircut. Must steam clean the carpet in the hall. I don't have the energy to administer another property, but disposal needs consideration.

After I had Crennan properly planted in the backyard, I turned off his phone and removed its SIM card. I didn't think anyone would be hunting for him too seriously yet, but I didn't want to take any chances. I then rewarded myself with a long, hot bath laced with a generous handful of Epsom salts, soaking off the sweat, dirt, and smell of underfelt. My day was by no means finished, of course, but I needed to rest. Before the day was out, I was hoping to pour the concrete slab and have it setting, which would mean a return to the hardware shop. I had a hallway which was still spattered with blood and shit to clean. I also had the small pile of Crennan's possessions to examine and dispose of. By the time the bath water was cooling sufficiently for me to face getting out, I had a plan of action: clean the hall as best I could; examine Crennan's possessions and see if I could work out who was so anxiously calling him; get to the hardware shop and buy or order the materials I needed for the concrete slab; get home in time to knock up the formwork for the slab.

The great benefit of a plan is that it allows action without thought, and I needed a bit of that. So, washed and refreshed, I armed myself with buckets, towels, washing cloths, ammonia, rubber gloves, and set to work to remove all traces of the Crennan/Furphy pas de deux. Kneeling was painful but the cleaning was easier than I thought, and although I didn't fool myself into thinking it would baffle forensic examination, it was soon good enough that I needn't fear the glances of any casual visitors. I was a little concerned at the smell of my faeces, as mentioned in my journal, and I suppose it was the sight of blood and faeces which suggested bowel cancer to my hypochondriacal mind; I resolved to commit to a bowel examination as soon as my life returned to normal.

The greater benefit of a plan is that, having postponed thought, it allows the subconscious to take charge. As I made my way into the living room, where I had my cache of Crennan's things, I realised that the hardware shop would have to wait for the morrow. I needed to get my hair cut. My subconscious was inexplicably interested in me being ready to assume Crennan's identity. I picked up Crennan's wallet and examined its contents. There was a surprising amount of cash: eleven hundred dollars, at least. It contained his driver's licence, his credit cards and bank cards, his police identification card. I slipped it into my pocket, promising I would spend his money as quickly and unwisely as I could.

I examined Crennan's pistol next. Not only was it loaded, the safety catch was off. The bastard had had every intention of killing me. I also realised that I could easily have fired off a round while I was bouncing on his chest. I found myself becoming angry at him all over again, the irresponsible git, but the thought of him lying face down in the dirt went some way to assuaging my anger. I put the pistol into the bottom drawer of Norma's desk. I've always thought it would be useful to have a handgun. They shorten arguments.

Interesting as the pistol was, it was the keys which really set me thinking. I had a set of Crennan's house keys, which would be handy while I organised his disappearance, but I also had his car keys. That meant that Crennan's car was probably parked in front of my house. As soon as his colleagues became curious about his whereabouts, his car would be the first thing they'd look for. My subconscious mind had recognised the need for a haircut before all else, but now my conscious mind overruled

More housework; more history

that. I had to take his car back to his house as soon as possible. I gave myself a quick once-over in the bathroom mirror to check that I bore no obvious traces of past activities. I went back to Norma's desk and picked up Crennan's mobile phone and SIM card, intending to reassemble them and leave them inside his house, then headed out to find his car.

I walked out the front gate and started clicking the electronic key. Bingo! His black Audi, a couple of years old, but lovingly smothered in polish, responded with a servile blink of its lights. Naturally, Crennan's car had the usual accessories of the inadequate male: fancy wheel trim, tinted windows, a wholly unnecessary spoiler. I climbed in behind the wheel, readjusted mirrors, and stopped. Fingerprints. I checked in the glovebox, expecting to find an over-priced vinyl-protection spray. Double bingo! A half-full spray bottle of Armourall Protectant ("UVA *and* UVB Sun Protection for your car!") and a cannister of moist wipes. I was surprised he didn't have nappy rash cream for it as well. Now confident that I could remove my fingerprints from his car, I started it up and pulled out into the road. For all my scorn for Crennan and his car, I have to say it was a significant improvement on driving Betsy. Not that I'd ever tell her.

I began navigating my way back to Crennan's house. My intention was to park it as close to his house as possible and then make my way home by public transport. As I was driving there, however, I worried about being seen getting out of his car. Perhaps my subconscious had a point. If I had a Crennan haircut, chances are that anyone spotting me would take me for Crennan himself.

I drove to the nearest, large shopping centre and went in search of a barber. Silly me. I needed a hairdresser, of course. I found Otto Raymond's Hair Design—a l'Oréal Professionel, if you don't mind—and trusted myself to Otto and his gals.

Two hours later, I emerged with the hair clipped short around most of my skull, the hair on the top left longer, and the hair in the middle of the top of my head swept up into a little cockscomb of stupidity. I kept my eyes on the ground and hurried back to the Audi. Once inside, I examined myself closely in the rear vision mirror. It was truly awful. But at least I looked like I belonged in an Audi. I drove directly to Crennan's house and parked in front. I spent ten minutes risking my lungs with the Armourall protectant spray, wiping down every internal surface of the car. I wiped down the spray bottle and returned it to the glovebox. I had a dozen used wipes to dispose of, and, rejoicing in the pain it would have caused Crennan, I stuffed them in the glovebox and shut it.

As I stood next to his car, I realised I had his house keys with me and that he wouldn't have had the chance to reinstall an alarm. It seemed an ideal time to check the house. I reasoned that anyone who saw me would think that Crennan had come home and I could duck out the back through the garage to make my escape. As it happened, the person who did see me going into the house thought exactly that.

I walked up to the familiar door, knocked and waited to make sure there was no one inside. Quiet as the grave. I unlocked the door and stepped inside, not observing the police car that was just arriving, and shut the door behind me. I smiled to see the mess that I'd made of the alarm in the hall and began a cautious reconnaissance of the house.

A loud thumping on the front door made me jump.

"Scott! Scott! Open up!"

I stood frozen in the hall, my gut churning with fear.

More hammering on the door.

"Scotty, I know you're in there! What's going on? Open up!"

I walked gingerly up to the front door.

"Who is it?" I asked, my voice hoarse.

"Scott? It's me, Gary," the exasperated voice explained. "I've been trying to call you. Open up. We've got a problem," he added urgently.

More housework; more history

"Can't, Gary," I whispered throatily. "Feeling shit." Which was probably true.

"Jesus, Scott. Peterson knows you've taken your sidearm with you. He's fuckin' livid. Where've you been?"

The gun. Of course. Crennan would have expected to return it to the station before anyone knew it was missing.

"Okay," I croaked. "Tell him I'll come in later."

"When?"

"Later today. An hour. Explain then."

The voice on the other side of the door was clearly not sure.

"You better, Scott. He's wild."

I made a grunt of assent.

"You sure you're okay? I can tell him you're okay?"

"Sure. Later."

"Okay. Call me if you need anything."

I listened to the cop turn slowly around and step off the verandah. I waited to hear the gate and the car drive off. It was difficult to hear anything above the sound of my heart trying to bash its way out of my chest. I crept back to the kitchen and drank handfuls of water from the tap. Gradually, I calmed down and allowed my brain to re-engage.

The situation, from what I could reasonably assume, was that Crennan had taken his firearm out of the station and it had been missed. His commanding officer—the estimable Peterson— was on the warpath and presumably, Crennan would be in for a bollocking once he returned. Well, I'd saved him from that. But when he didn't turn up at all today, they'd start a more vigorous search for him. I needed to provide a deadend for them to explore. The only deadend I could think of was Adelaide.

Adelaide: an hour's flight away in a different state and a different time zone: 1950. It had no connection to me, Crennan, or Sabasa as far as I knew. I began leaving a very obvious trail.

More housework; more history

I reassembled Crennan's phone and SIM card and rang Qantas and booked an expensive one way ticket to Adelaide, leaving in just over two hours' time, paid with Crennan's credit card. I rang a taxi and arranged to be picked up in thirty minutes. Then I went to Crennan's bedroom and found a small suitcase and packed a few days' clothes. I was pleased to see that he'd been sleeping in a sleeping bag on top of his ruined bed. I left other clothes spread out on the bed as if he'd been making a selection. What else would he need? Shoes. I threw a pair of runners into the bag. Toiletries. I went to the bathroom and took his toothbrush, toothpaste, and electric razor. I went to kitchen where I'd seen a notepad on the fridge and wrote the flight number and time and 'Adelaide' in block letters. I wondered if my handwriting looked anything like Crennan's and then reflected that even if the cops thought it was someone else's writing, that would only add to the mystery. I sat and waited for the taxi to honk. I flicked through the call history in Crennan's phone and found a dozen calls from someone called 'Gazza', whom I took to be the exasperated colleague, Gary. I'd send Gazza a text from Adelaide.

When the taxi arrived, I made a great show of being in a hurry. I was curt to the driver and continually pressed him to hurry. I made sure to question him several times about the route he was taking. When we got to the airport, I paid with Crennan's credit card. As I was getting out of the cab, I slipped Crennan's police identification card out of his wallet and left it on the back seat for the next passenger to find and hand to the driver.

I turned to the driver, "Listen. You forget you ever took me on this trip, okay? You never saw my face."

To his credit, the driver gave me look of scornful contempt and dismissed me with a flick of his hand. I slammed the door and headed into the terminal, catching sight of my reflection and was momentarily embarrassed by the ridiculous haircut I now sported. I checked in, asking that the small bag, which I might have taken on as hand luggage, be weighed and checked through to Adelaide.

The flight to Adelaide was as uneventful as one hopes when flying. I arrived in Adelaide and went straight to an ATM where I withdrew a $1000 cash advance from Crennan's card. Then I bought a bus ticket into the city, leaving the bag to circle endlessly on the baggage carousel. As I headed to the bus, I caught sight of a security camera. I knew the image it captured would be too indistinct to allow the cops to say I wasn't Crennan, but I thought I should give them something more to think about. I walked over to a solidly built, impressively tattooed Islander who was dragging a large suitcase behind him.

"Excuse me," I started politely, "but I think you have my bag."

"What?" he looked at me puzzled.

"That's my bag you've got."

"No…" but before he could get any further, I bent down, ostensibly to look at the luggage tickets on the case.

I stood up.

"Sorry. My mistake."

I hurried to the bus stop, leaving a mildly irritated Islander behind me. I hoped that would give the police something to think about when they began to wonder who I was meeting and what I was doing in Adelaide. On the bus, I pulled out Crennan's phone and wrote a short text to Gazza: "Sorry, mate. Had to go. Call you in a couple of weeks. All good." I was about to send it when I thought to check previous messages he'd sent. I reformatted it to suit his texting style: "Soz mate had to go. fucked up call u soon".

I got off the bus near Rundle Mall and began looking for a hotel. The Paringa Motel looked suitably budget-friendly and the name somehow reminded me of Norma and her Onkaparinga blankets. I booked a Deluxe room, paying with a hundred of Crennan's cash, but using my own credit card for identification. Crennan had reached Adelaide airport, but he'd now disappeared for good. I bought a toothbrush from the reception, explaining that my luggage had got lost but should turn up tomorrow. The smart, young man on the desk expressed just enough sympathy to communicate his complete lack of interest in whether I had luggage or not.

I went straight up to my room. It was only early evening, but I was exhausted. I had started in Melbourne, burying a body, and ended up 450 miles away, feeling as though I ought to be buried myself. I lay on the bed and fell asleep. I awoke about ten o'clock that night and had a shower and brushed my teeth. I considered calling room service for a sandwich, but I wasn't hungry. I made myself a cup of tasteless, hot brown water using two of the tired looking teabags supplied. The colour may have come from Adelaide's tap water, of course. I lay on the bed, allowing myself to wonder what Sabasa was doing and when I was going to see her again. I also started thinking about how I could convince her that Crennan had left our lives forever.

Gradually, my pleasant reverie about Sabasa and the gentle, loving future we shared, gave way to thoughts of morality. Murder always raises some sort of moral question, I find. Morality led to religion; the specific—my despatching of Crennan—led to the general and I jotted down a few ideas for my sadly neglected political work.

Ensuring Religious Freedom in Australia

Extract from A Programme of Moderate Political Reform in Australia, www.pmpra.com

Any programme of moderate political reform in Australia must address the question of religious freedom. It is an assumption in Australia, a convention, that we should be free to choose our religion and practice our religious beliefs, but this is not guaranteed. There is certainly provision in the Constitution to ensure that the Commonwealth does not make any law which prohibits 'the free exercise of any religion' or which requires particular religious adherence to any office or public trust, but is that truly religious freedom?

There is nothing in our constitution or in the legislatures of the states of the Commonwealth to prevent the government of the day favouring one religion over another. When you consider how powerful government favour can be, is this something we should continue to allow?

We cannot achieve the separation of religion and state while we have a state religion, but it is not enough simply to abandon our nominal Anglican state religion. If we believe in a complete separation of religion and state, we should ensure that government keeps out of religion entirely. The state should have nothing to say about God or the practices of worshipping God, with one important proviso: religious adherence cannot be allowed to circumvent the laws of the land. A 'religion' might condone a marriage between a seven year old girl and a forty-five year old man, or it might call for human sacrifice on the full moon, but the law applies to all and overrides all religious customs or concerns. Beyond that, government has no business telling anyone what their god or gods are, say, do, or require, as long as those practices are not in conflict with the laws of the land.

The only way to ensure religious freedom is to abolish all mention and consideration of it in all our legislation. Quite simply, government should not recognise religion at all. We should remove all references to religion and god from all legislation. There should be no tax benefits for religions or churches—because that empowers government to dictate what is a valid religion and what is not. There should be no distinction made between funding for schools beyond the sensible distribution of funds to all Australian children equally. Government should stop its surreptitious funding of some religions with tax breaks and other concessions, and get out of the god business altogether.

Government doesn't bother trying to recognise other pastimes, why should it concern itself with religion? Why should people who want to gather together to drone about God be treated any differently from people in a book club who want to inflict their opinions about literature on each other? Citizens in a free country must be allowed to organise their lives with as little interference from government as is practical.

Introducing freedom of religion by dissociating government from it entirely will allow those who want to construct or occupy temples or churches in which to worship the freedom to conduct themselves according to their religions, paying all the appropriate rates and taxes, finally comfortable in the knowledge that are not imposing on their fellow citizens. It removes the ever-present stigma of bludging from all religions, and it simultaneously removes the stigma that some religious people are currently made to suffer because their set of beliefs is judged to be 'not a religion' by a secular government with no expertise or religious authority to do so.

There is no reason for government to recognise religion: it adds nothing to the religion. God does not require it. In order to ensure true freedom of religion, we must remove all reference to it in all our laws and legal documents.

© Copyright 2016, Thom Furphy

Postcard

> Postcard from Sabasa! She ignored radio silence and I'm unable to feel anything other than delight. Kev's retreat has worked its lunatic magic. Start planning for her return.

Wisely, I didn't record anything in my journal about my dash to Adelaide. I flew back on a budget flight under my own name. I had flattened my hair in the morning under the shower and had dressed in yesterday's t-shirt and trousers, leaving the shirt I had worn as Crennan behind in the hotel. I hoped my appearance was different enough that, even if the cops were dedicated enough to review several days of airport CCTV footage, they wouldn't tag me as Crennan.

I arrived back in Melbourne around midday. I had meant to dispose of Crennan's remaining possessions—keys, cards, wallet—in Adelaide, but I had ended up bringing them back to Melbourne with me. I regretted that I hadn't emptied Crennan's bank account so I could give its contents to Sabasa, but I reflected that as I had accidentally kept his cards, I could hold onto them for a couple of months. The police would monitor his accounts over the coming weeks, no doubt, to try to find evidence of his whereabouts, but eventually their interest in him would give way to other priorities and perhaps I would yet be able to redirect his money to Sabasa. I even played with the idea of assuming proprietorial control of Crennan's house, but reluctantly came to the conclusion that I couldn't safely take any further advantage of the Senior Constable. I still had about $1500 of his cash, as well as a police handgun, a computer wrapped in carpet, an unfinished DIY project in the backyard, and a few, very unpleasant memories. That was plenty.

Once home, I made myself tea and crumpets. I had a punnet of tired looking raspberries in the fridge; so I microwaved them for a few minutes with half a cup of sugar and had hot raspberry jam on my crumpets. It was reviving. I decided that Crennan's memorial stone was my priority for the day. I spent half an hour looking up how to mix cement, sand, and screening into concrete and how to estimate the amounts of each needed. I made a list of the things I needed to buy, and then went out to the backyard to knock up the formwork to hold the wet concrete.

I had plenty of spare palings and wooden stakes and in half an hour or so, I had a solid framework built and ready for the concrete. I was noticeably stiff bending and straightening, and my knee was troubling me, but I had no choice but to press on. Despite knowing how much it would hurt Barry, I wasn't going to bother with screenings and sand beneath this small slab. I would simply lie a rectangle of steel mesh reinforcing on the soil and pour the concrete over it. I would need to have the steel mesh cut to size; so I measured the final interior rectangle of the formwork to make sure I got the right size. As I was bent over Crennan I had an altogether unnecessary thought. I scrabbled around under the nearby shrubs and found some dry twigs. I broke them into convenient sizes and used the pieces of twig to spell out in mirror writing 'HELP'. My screamingly funny idea was that, by the time anyone lifted the slab, the twigs would be long gone and all they'd see was a message apparently scratched from below on the concrete. Well, it amused me at the time.

After a trip to the hardware shop and a steady afternoon's work, the sun and the concrete were setting over Crennan. I sat next to Norma's pond, sipping a celebratory beer, basking, for one of the very few occasions of my life, in the glow of hard, physical work well done. I felt sore and tired, but pleased with my efforts.

My rewards were not over. I had spent a busy day, neglecting the many small, everyday tasks which usually composed my days. As I walked inside to make myself dinner, I remembered that I hadn't checked the letterbox. I set a saucepan of water to boil, then went to the letterbox and found it: a postcard from Sabasa! I studied the reproduction of an old painting of Hobart harbour, Mount Wellington shrouded in the smoke of a steamer in the background, too excited to turn the card over and read her words. When I did convince myself to turn the card, I studied her handwriting without reading the words. I don't know what I expected, but I was relieved that her handwriting was closer to Itálica or Redonda than Cortesana or, heaven forbid, Procesal. Finally, I convinced myself to read her words.

"Dear Thom,

"I am so happy here! I can never thank you enough. The ashram is wonderful (Shushan doesn't cook as well as you, though!) and Fiona and I are the only guests. I am alive again, Thom! Alive! I can't thank you enough. Call me. Your 'Sab' XXX"

I just kept reading it over and over. She likes my cooking! Your Sab. *Your Sab!* And then three kisses. I walked slowly back into the house, not hurrying, even as I heard the water boiling over and hissing on the gas hob. Three kisses will do that.

I want to describe my feelings that evening, but I find it difficult. I am very distant from that time, a different person. I had been working hard, physically, and I had been under considerable mental strain as well, and being relieved of both at the same time must have contributed to a heightening of sensation. I was elated. The relief of having delivered myself of the past several days was combined with an overwhelming explosion of love for Sabasa. I felt myself suffused with chemical magic. I was lighter; colours were brighter; the air was like a soft, warm blanket around me. I had only to think of her face, her deep, dark eyes looking back at me, and I began to smile, to feel a new rush of love for her course through my body. I was awash with love for her. I saw her perfection, whole, and I saw her perfections, singular. If I had known of faults or blemishes, I could only have seen their faultlessness, their beauty. I saw how everything about her contributed to her beauty. I wanted to count her perfections so I could taste them in my mouth. I wanted to hear her voice, her laugh which, even as I remembered it, could cause me to gasp with pleasure. Her voice was as beautiful as birdsong, as beautiful and sibilant as the sound of tree leaves shaken by a breeze or by a bird. Her words, her writing caressed the paper like warm hands on my skin. I surrendered myself to my love for her. Before that evening, I had kept myself in check. I knew I was intrigued by her. I knew I admired her. Now, I abandoned myself to her. I was besotted, drunk, high, lost in recurring waves of love for her. I allowed myself love and I allowed no way out.

I sat reading and re-reading, dreaming and re-dreaming. I finally began to feel cold and took myself off to bed.

Dr No's student days

> Love hurts. All over. Visit to doctor unhelpful.

Long acquaintance with Hollywood movies and drippy American television led me to believe I would waken to sunshine, birdsong, and an elevated mood. I expected to spin out of bed and burst into a song about the wonders of being in love.

I could barely move.

My chest was congested, my head ached, and when I swung my legs out of bed, I found I could hardly stand. My joints, particularly my bruised knee, seemed to have seized up. Everything, every part of my body, ached. I struggled through the morning, drinking a pot of Sri Lankan tea with milk and sugar, but not able to face cooking porridge or any more substantial breakfast. Reluctantly, I made an appointment to see Dr No that afternoon, and then returned to bed, where I slept uncomfortably, alternately overheated and sweating or shivering uncontrollably, unable to warm myself.

At two thirty, the alarm I had set rang to warn me to get to the doctor's. I struggled out of bed and into yesterday's clothes, limped out to Betsy, and drove to Dr No's, a journey I would normally walk in ten minutes.

"Not booked in yet for psychotherapy?" was Dr No's cheery greeting. "Erection problems persisting?"

"I haven't thought about erections," I answered truthfully.

"No, because you have a real medical problem to worry about." Dr No cast his diagnostic eye over me. "You feel sore?"

"All over," I wheezed.

"Throat, chest congested?"

I nodded miserably.

"Virus. Common cold, probably. Influenza, possibly. At your age you should start thinking about 'flu shots every year."

"My joints ache. All over."

"The miracle of the influenza virus. Examination. Shirt off, singlet off."

I undressed clumsily and let Dr No tap, harumph, listen, and pronounce.

"Excellent diagnosis, Dr No," he congratulated himself. "Bed rest, lots of fluids, lots of sleep." Antibiotics only if chest doesn't clear up. Make an appointment for next week."

He seemed about to dismiss me well inside the six minutes of consultation he needed to observe to make a living.

"What about my joints?"

"Aching joints a very common symptom of influenza. Panadol if needed. No more than eight tablets per day."

"No, I think I've injured my knee," I persisted. "It's very painful and swollen. I hit it," I finished weakly.

"Trousers off," commanded Dr No.

I struggled out of my trousers and was surprised at how swollen and bruised my knee was. For the first time in the consultation, Dr No looked interested. He examined the knee closely, gently feeling the bruising and looking closely at the bruise marks.

"Very interesting. Significant bruising," he looked at me quizzically. "I have only once seen similar."

"I fell on a stone, I think," I offered.

"Fell on a stone? You think?" he paused, and drew a ballpoint pen out of his pocket. With the end of the pen, he began tracing the pattern of the bruise. "Stone injury? Dr No says, 'No!' No, Mr Furphy, I have seen this pattern before in Malaysia. On the cheek of a young man who had not answered police enquiries satisfactorily."

He paused, looking at me intently, waiting for a response. I remained silent, not know what he was expecting. He turned his attention back to my knee and continued his examination.

"This," he traced an outer ring of bruising, "looks like the trigger guard of a gun. And this," he traced the small crescent within the ring, "is the trigger."

Dr No looked directly into my eyes.

"The student I attended had a pistol slammed into his face by an impatient interrogator. You have fallen, Mr Furphy, onto a gun, not a stone."

"Oh, that's it!" I responded feebly, "The kids' party. Bit of rough and tumble in the backyard and I knelt too heavily, fell really, onto one of the toy guns. That explains it."

Dr No nodded sagely. "That would indeed explain it."

He started looking behind him and came back to the examination couch with a roll of elastic bandage.

"That would explain it if an idiot was explaining it to another idiot."

He began strapping my knee.

"But one of us, is not an idiot. Rest is the only requirement at this stage. We will examine it again in a week."

I wrestled my legs back into my trousers and pulled on my t-shirt and shirt. Dr No went to his desk and began making notes. He dismissed me curtly.

"Make an appointment for next week. I have to write my notes."

I limped my way to the door of the examination room.

"Thanks, Dr No," I turned and mumbled.

He looked up from his notes and said quietly, "I do not approve of guns, Mr Furphy."

There was something about the tone of his voice which alerted me to an obvious fact: Dr No was far more dangerous than

Crennan had ever been. I limped out to the reception to make my next appointment, wondering how seriously I needed to worry about Dr No.

That evening, I made a few more notes for Norma's biography, but my heart wasn't in it. There was something ominous in Dr No's tone.

Family history

Extract from "Bridge of Generations, the unauthorised biography of Norma Selfe", unpublished

Although not well known in Victoria, the Selfe family name was highly regarded in neighbouring New South Wales. Norma's grandfather, Norman Selfe, after whom she had been named, was one of the most famous and influential engineers and architects in the flourishing colony. The Sydney suburb of Normanhurst is named after him. In his long and distinguished career, Norman Selfe was responsible for many innovations and inventions, including devices to clear and dredge Sydney harbour, the first commercial refrigeration plant in the southern hemisphere, and, of course, a winning design for the Sydney Harbour Bridge.

The prize won by Norman Selfe in 1902 for designing the Harbour Bridge was not the first prize he'd won for the bridge—he'd come second in 1900 with a design for a suspension bridge. None of the designs of that earlier competition had been selected for building, however, and a second competition was concluded in 1902. Selfe's design, an elegant, triple arched bridge supported by four pylons was selected as the winner. After the death of her parents in 1963, Norma had the architectural drawing of the winning design framed and it was displayed proudly on her living room wall, next to her own award for Dental Prosthetics, which, as she would archly comment, was for her improvements to the design of dental bridges.[9] Unlike

---

[9] The Selfe Bridge is still one of the most commonly fitted dental bridge designs used in Australia. Norma published her design without the protection of any patent and has consequently never received any remuneration for the tens of thousands of mouths which unknowingly carry her work.

Norma's bridge, Norman Selfe's Sydney Harbour Bridge was not built and the city had to wait another thirty years for its bridge.

Norma never married. She continued a lifelong correspondence with Clarence Fong, occasionally visiting him after his retirement, but there is no record of any other close attachment. She never heard from her Joe, accepting that he must have returned to Italy, or found a new life somewhere else in Australia. In her final years, she dreamt of receiving a letter from her son, a letter saying he had tracked her down through the adoption agency records and wanted to meet her. She read about such things happening and saw occasional reunions on the television. She kept a small notebook of her life to give to him to help him understand. No letter ever came.

© Copyright 2016, Thom Furphy

I decided to call the Ashram that evening to talk to Sabasa. I needed to hear her voice and to tell her it was safe to return as soon as she wanted to. The phone was answered by a female voice, and after I'd told her who I was and asked to speak to Sabasa, she replied,

"So you're the wonderful Thom!"

"Ah, yes. That's me," I confirmed, awkwardly.

"Fiona. I'm staying at the ashram with Claire. Claire's gone on and on about you!"

I may have blushed with happiness.

"Is she there? I wanted a quick word."

"Sorry, Thom, she's off buying supplies with Shushan, but they won't be too long if you want to call back."

"That's all right," I lied, crushed. "I'm not feeling too flash; I'll probably be asleep in ten minutes. Could you tell her I called?"

"Of course."

"And tell Kev—Shushan, sorry—that I'm thinking of coming down myself in a day or two, just for a quick catch up."

"Great, Thom. I'm really looking forward to meeting you. Claire says you saved her life."

"She's a dag," I finished, weakly. "Thanks for taking the messages, Fiona. See you in a day or two."

I hung up the phone, the hollow feeling of disappointment at not having heard Sabasa's voice was unexpected and painful. I realised that part of my need for hearing her was my continuing worry about Dr No. And I didn't know why. But something was nagging me. I had a need to simplify the situation.

I went to my desk and fished out the handgun. I sprayed it with window cleaner and wiped it carefully with cloth. When I was satisfied that it would show no fingerprints, I put it in a large, manila envelope and wrote 'Gaz' in block letters on the front. I sealed the envelope, placed it in a plastic bag, and took it out to the car.

I drove to Crennan's house, stopping fifty metres shy of his gate. I turned off the engine and inspected every car in the street, looking for anything that might be a police car. They were all unremarkably suburban with no occupants. I got out of Betsy with the envelope and strolled towards his front gate, whistling quietly. I searched every house, every garden, every window for any sign of any watcher. As I approached the front gate, I gave one more look around, and then, using the plastic bag to protect the envelope from my fingerprints, I stuffed the envelope into Crennan's letterbox. I turned smartly and walked back to Betsy as carelessly jauntily as I could. I suspect I looked like an inexpertly operated marionette, limping awkwardly.

Nervous, feverish, and exhausted, I drove home.

I went to pick up Crennan's phone, intending to send Gaz a text, but remembered that Crennan was meant to be in Adelaide and I didn't want any phone records in Melbourne. I loaded the SIM card into his phone, copied Gaz's number onto a piece of paper, then turned off the phone and removed the SIM card again. Then I turned on the mobile I'd bought to call Crennan and sent a text from it to Gaz.

"Gaz, Scott C. New phone. Go to my letterbox. Missing item in envelope. Tell them will come in mon and explain. Thanks m8".

I turned off the phone before Gaz or anyone else could call it. I took out the SIM card and dropped it and both phones into the kitchen bin.

I knew the issue which would be causing all the froth and bubble at Richmond station was the missing firearm. I assumed that once they had that back under lock and key, the desire to find Crennan would lessen and no one would be anxious to draw attention to the handgun having taken a few days unpaid leave, particularly as they'd be able to establish that it hadn't been fired recently. Gaz would probably be appalled that Crennan had left the firearm in a letterbox, but that would merely hasten his efforts to retrieve it. Once they had it back and under control, they could concentrate on providing proper support and counselling for their colleague before quietly dismissing him. Except, of course, he wouldn't present himself for sympathy or sacking.

I then sat at the desk, logged on to a travel site, and booked a return ticket to Tasmania, leaving in a couple of days and returning on the day following. I was still feeling poorly, so I poured myself a tot of Norma's preferred blended whisky, added a squeeze of lemon and a drop of hot water, and took myself off to bed.

Love is declared

> Reunion with Sabasa. Stayed with Kevin in a newly completed mud hive. Surprisingly comfortable. Community dinner with Kev, Sab, Fiona, each contributing a course...

The visit to the ashram is difficult for me to write about. I want to start at the end of the visit, but the chronology of this story is confusing enough, I suppose.

I spent a couple of days in bed, and although not fully recovered, I felt well enough to travel. I rang Kevin from Melbourne airport in the morning to let him know what time my flight got in. I was expecting to have to pay a taxi to ferry me out to the ashram, but Kevin volunteered to pick me up. He didn't, of course. I was greeted at Hobart by Sabasa who rushed forward as I entered the arrivals area, hugged me around the neck, and planted a kiss on my cheek.

"Thom! Thank you for coming! I'm so happy to see you!"

I took a moment drinking in the sight. She looked smaller than I remembered, but so beautiful! And she shone. You will think this is the standard hyperbole of an affected lover, but I am describing my experience in scientifically precise and objective terms: she shone with happiness. Her eyes, her smile, shone, her body was electric, like a puppy seeing its master. She was alive with happiness.

She took my arm and steered me towards a pleasant looking woman in Indian clothing.

"This is Fiona," she announced, grinning. "Fiona's driving us back to Shushan in her car."

Fiona was older than Sabasa. Her hair was cut short and dyed a rich auburn. I reached out a hand to shake hers and noticed that she wasn't at all 'pleasant looking'. She was striking. She had a deep, calm, natural beauty, but you had to observe her to

Love is declared

see it. She smiled shyly as she took my hand, looking into my eyes. Her eyes smiled without a hint of shyness.

"I'm really proud to meet you, Thom."

"Proud?" I asked awkwardly.

Fiona caught my awkwardness and blushed slightly, "Well, you know, Claire described you... everything you've done."

I made a non-committal, heroic plosive sound—a syllable I hoped would convey 'Yes, I am something of a hero, but it was something that any one of a dozen heroes might have done. Had they been there. They weren't, of course. I did it. I did it all. Just me.'

Sabasa gave my arm a squeeze and said, "Well, I've never been happier. Let's get to the car."

I was travelling only with a small carry-on bag; so we went straight to Fiona's car—an old HG Ute with one bench seat. I threw my bag into the back and we all climbed into the cab: Fiona driving, Sabasa in the middle, me riding shotgun. As I climbed into the cabin, Sabasa turned to me, laughing.

"What's happened to your hair?"

I'd forgotten the Crennan haircut. The dorsal-fin-look required that you put product in your hair to stiffen it and then comb it into its ridiculous little crest after every shower. Naturally, I'd just let it lie flat. The result was an unflattering little runway of hair falling in an indistinct strip on the top of my head.

"I was in a hurry cutting it," I lied.

"But you've clipped the rest of your hair very neatly," she insisted, before sensing my confusion. "Don't worry. Fiona and I will find some scissors and see what we can do to fix it."

"Thanks," I offered, desperate for another topic of conversation to take over. "The ute's unexpected, Fiona."

She leant around Sabasa and smiled at me. "You'll find I'm a very practical girl."

Love is declared

The trip to the ashram passed happily enough after that. I told a few stories of Kevin and the establishment of the ashram and of his misadventures with fellow seekers of enlightenment; Sabasa and Fiona told gently humorous stories of Shushan's current treatments and baffling philosophy.

"But," said Fiona, "you cannot fault the place as a resting place to recharge the batteries. It's really very beautiful."

We turned off the main road towards a ridge of hills and I could see the trees of the ashram lining the driveway. I hadn't been there for seven or eight years, and I was impressed with how established, how settled it looked. The winding driveway, which I had helped Kevin lay, grubbing out recalcitrant messmate roots, was now lined with mature bottlebrush, wattles, eucalypts, and a straggly-looking cypress hedge, which turned out to be Kevin's attempt to grow a stand of Huon Pines. In a thousand years, he may have done it, of course. The ashram itself was now a substantial collection of mud brick buildings, grouped around the central building I had helped Kevin build. I could see it had had several additions over the years, but its slow, organic growth made it look very much a part of the natural landscape.

As we pulled into the ashram, Kevin came out to meet us. He embraced me with the warmth of a man whom few other men understood. I returned his embrace in the happy knowledge that I was not one of that tiny band.

"Mate!" He stood back to look at me before sweeping his arm around behind him to indicate the ashram. "What do you think of it?"

"It looks beautiful, Kev. I can't believe how well you've succeeded with it."

"WE. We succeeded, Thom." He turned to Sabasa and Fiona, "Thom was the first one here to help me. The first one to believe in my vision."

Love is declared

I made the appropriate disparaging noises and didn't enlighten anyone to my complete lack of belief in Kevin and his visions, then or now.

"Come on in. Let's get you settled in one of the hives."

We marched together to one of the small, mud brick dwellings which encircled the main building. Kevin had called them hives, and I could see the similarity. Each hut was circular with a single door and a couple of windows. The rooves were conical and shingled. The huts themselves looked like large, inverted coil pots. Kevin was watching my face to gauge my reaction. He must have seen a questioning look flit over my face. He pounced happily into conversation.

"I knew you'd be intrigued! Cylindrical mud bricks! No one else has made them, to my knowledge. I pack mud and straw into lengths of down pipes, stand them on end for a day or two, then push out a wet pipeline of mud which I can arrange in an arc for drying. I cut the mud pipes into bricks and let them dry. Then I use them to build my conical hives around a timber frame!"

"Wow. I'm impressed, Kev. Remember the trouble we had with the mud bricks for the original building?"

Kevin laughed at the memory: the aching weeks of mixing and drying the bricks; the inexpert brick laying; the sight of half a building dissolving in one downpour.

"I'm better at it now!"

We entered my hive. It was simply furnished: a bed, a chair and table, a cast iron pot belly stove. The floor was covered in rag rugs. The timber frame which supported the roof was left exposed. There were a couple of hand woven pieces of fabric on the walls as decoration. There was no electricity; candles and a kero hurricane lamp stood on the table with a box of matches beside them.

"Perfect, Kev."

Love is declared

I put my bag down. Kevin gave me another hug and then turned to the two women who'd followed us.

"Fiona, let's you and me finish making lunch and let Thom and Claire catch up."

I sat on the bed and Sabasa took the chair. She spoke first.

"I don't suppose we really have much to catch up about," she began. "I've only been gone a week and a couple of days, but it feels like years!"

"You look well."

It was a ridiculous statement. She looked wonderful. She looked as radiant as an icon Madonna, surrounded in a sea of gold leaf.

"I feel so *clean*, Thom. I can't tell you. I can't explain."

"You'll feel cleaner when I tell you that your ex problem is an ex-problem."

Her face changed instantly. The glow was replaced with a hard, pinched expression.

"I don't know if I want to think about it."

"You don't have to. Nothing to think about. Crennan has left the force, left his house, left the state. He knows he will end up in gaol if he ever contacts you again."

"Jail?"

"Gaol," I corrected. "I prefer the older spelling: g-a-o-l."

She smiled thinly. "Okay, Thom-with-an-aitch."

She became serious again.

"Where has he gone. He hasn't gone to Sydney? Or here?" she added.

"No. Your sister in Sydney is quite safe. As is Tasmania. He's moved to Adelaide and he will disappear from your life. Guaranteed. He thinks I have incriminating videos of him. I haven't. I've destroyed everything."

Love is declared

Sabasa grew thoughtful. It was several moments before she spoke.

"I…" she looked at me with a sad tenderness, "I don't know how to say this without sounding as if I'm ungrateful."

I smiled at her. "You don't need my permission to tell me anything, Sabasa. And I'm not looking for gratitude or applause or anything else. I offer only that which I seek: some human sympathy in this mysterious island."

"A quote?" she asked.

"Shelley. From an unfinished play. His best ones were all unfinished."

She nodded quietly and then continued.

"I don't know what you did or said or how you managed to have him move to Adelaide, and I know you will have been very clever and brave…" she paused and looked deeply into my eyes, "… and I don't care. I can't care. Coming here, I have freed myself. By myself. I know that sounds terrible. You paid for me, you convinced me, you told me about this place. I'm grateful for that Thom. I will always love you for that, Thom, but I *freed* myself from him by myself. *I* did it. I don't care about him. I'm not scared of him. I dismiss him. I have *cleaned* myself of him."

She looked to see if she had hurt me.

"Of course you did it. Only you could do it. You mustn't think I need to think I played any more than a bit part in this."

A flicker of annoyance passed over her face. "Of course you played more than a bit part. You were the reason I could free myself. You gave me the physical safety, the shell. You gave me the time, space, and resources to be able to free myself, but the act of removing him from my life, Thom, the act of shedding that snake skin of fear and dependence, *that's* the thing I did by myself."

She took my hands in hers.

Love is declared

"Do you understand me, Thom? I need you to understand me."

I wanted to go on holding her hands. I wanted her to keep looking into my eyes.

"I think I understand."

She nodded.

"Good. There's one more thing, Thom."

I waited.

"You'll think I'm mad. But I've had a lot of time here to think and I don't care whether people think I'm just rushing from one relationship to another, but I've had experience now, with you, of a life that is quiet and loving and safe, and I want to have that sort of life. I want to live like that and having found someone I can live with, I want to try to live that life."

She looked at me with tears welling in her eyes.

"No one will think you're rushing. Your heart is rejoicing in its freedom. You owe it to yourself to allow yourself to love and to be loved."

I couldn't speak any further. My throat tightened and my mouth went dry. I was overwhelmed with a great wave of love and longing for this strong, fragile, beautiful woman. I wanted to take her in my arms and hold her against me. All my dreams of living with her, sharing our lives in a warm cocoon of love, flooded over me.

Sabasa looked up and saw I was unable to say more. She squeezed my hands, lowered her head shyly and whispered, "Thank you, Thom. I knew you would understand. I know it's too fast to be sure, but I don't need to be sure. I love the life I think we can have together. I really think I might love her."

So this is how it feels

> *...Now I know how it feels to have one's chest crushed. Incapable of breathing, but still alive. Lunch was tasteless. Great food, probably, but without taste. May have lost all physical senses. New haircut. Return to Melbourne hardly a return: a reversion.*

I wasn't looking at Sabasa when she used the wrong pronoun. I was holding her hands, looking down, afraid I might cry with happiness. When she said, "I really think I might love her," I felt nothing at first. Then the nothing I felt began to spread. I began to feel nothing all over. My head was blank. The air left my lungs without my exhaling. The feeling in my hands left me. My whole body began to dissociate, to dissolve into individual atoms of nothingness, began to disperse through the air. I began nodding gently, still not looking up, hoping this rhythmic muscle spasm might appear normal, might prevent me betraying myself, might restore me my body, my control. I saw Crennan below me as I crushed the wind out of his lungs, the life out of his body, and I became Crennan.

Sabasa wasn't looking at me. She was still happily telling me of her wonder at finding Fiona.

"It was sort of instant, Thom. I've never believed in love at first sight, but it was an instant attraction, affection. I had this instant affinity with her. She smiled at me when Shushan introduced us, and lights ignited through my body. I could suddenly see how my life might be. I felt like a girl again!"

She paused and I could tell she was looking up at me. I was still nodding, still staring at her hands.

"I know it sounds mad. It is mad, Thom. It's a type of madness, but I don't care. I want to live in this new type of madness. It's given me myself back. I want to live in it, at least for a while."

She paused again, uncertain.

"Thom?"

I murmured something and raised my face to look at her. I tried to smile, but I must have looked like the cadaver I had become. Sabasa's face distorted with pain and concern.

"Thom, are you all right? Is this okay for me to tell you?"

"Of course," I heard a voice that could have passed for mine tell her.

"Thom," she looked deeply into my eyes, her voice becoming softened with her concern, "are you sure you're all right? Thom? You didn't think..."

Mercifully, she didn't complete her question, but the question haunted her eyes.

"Please, Sabasa, of course you can tell me," the disembodied voice continued. I may even have been able to contort my face into a semblance of a smile.

Sabasa dropped her gaze again.

"Anyway, I wanted you to know. I wanted you to know how much you've done for me."

She gently let go of my hands.

"I'll leave you to unpack and help with the lunch."

She stood and went to leave the hive. As she reached the door, she turned and added, "I will always love you for what you've done, Thom."

I smiled and nodded and she turned and left.

'You didn't think...' the words returned to me. I did think. I had thought. I did think.

I stood slowly and looked around the room. There was a small mirror placed above the table and I caught sight of myself. The ludicrousness of what I had thought pierced me, stake through the heart, knife between the ribs, pin through the abdomen. The sad, the wretched man with the absurd haircut looked out at me. That ridiculous man, that grotesque caricature of a man, that imbecile with the sad, lined, face, he had thought... That a woman like Sabasa might... That such a woman could... Yes, he had thought it. He *had* thought. Fool.

I slumped back down on the bed. I closed my eyes, hoping I would never need to open them again.

*

The deceit of Self in the male

Extract from the unpublished work, 'Masculinear', by Thomas Furphy

The male brain is incapable of any reasonable understanding of self. For men, 'self' encompasses, includes, the world in which the male acts. It is not restricted to the component within the world which others might call that person, that 'self'. This is why, when referring to the male idea of 'self', I prefer to use the term Self, with an initial capital letter.

This is not the case for women who have an instinctive understanding of 'self' and 'other', perhaps the result of biology and their role in the production of 'other', but men are without this awareness. Men can accommodate the same logical position, of course, which is why so many women remain ignorant of the male blindness to self, but this accommodation does not extend as far as understanding. Every man will claim that an understanding of 'self' and 'other' is clear and self-evident and will dismiss the possibility of confusion or uncertainty, but they are mistaken.

For men, the 'other' only exists as 'an other to my Self'. The 'other' only exists, therefore, in opposition to Self. When the constructed world of the male Self is threatened or when it collapses, crushed by the weight of reality upon its beams of wishful fantasy, the male Self faces oblivion.

*

"Thom?"

I was awoken by Kevin. I had fallen asleep after Sabasa's announcement and Kev had come to fetch me to lunch.

"Come on, old boy!" he jollied me upright, and off the bed. "Lunch is ready in the pod. You must have been tired to fall asleep like that!"

I tried to smile drowsily and not at all like a man who had been eviscerated by love. "Yes, I've had a busy few days."

Kevin led me to the pod, extolling the food that had been prepared for this lunch.

"The ladies really wanted to make something special for you! They haven't let me do more than mix some salad dressing."

We entered the pod together. A long, central table was decorated with a pulled thread embroidered linen table cloth, bowls of food, and sprays of foliage and flowers. Fiona and Sabasa stood behind the table, beaming with pride, love, and the shared joy of each other's company. The hollowness in my gut expanded to become a universe of dark matter.

"Wow!" I exclaimed with the inexpert actor's usual mixture of too much volume and too little conviction. "What a fabulous looking feast!"

Kevin led me to a slab chair, messmate and redgum, then stood at the head of the table and pronounced a peculiar grace.

"We join together in witness of the bounty, the beauty, the blessing that we share. We have received all and we share all. Friends, we celebrate with food and drink and fellowship. Shalom!"

I didn't know if we were expected to respond to the idiosyncratic use of Hebrew to end the grace, but I muttered an inaudible syllable as we all sat to table.

The meal was probably fabulous. It had certainly taken them hours to prepare. It was no one's fault that I couldn't taste anything. I chewed and swallowed and made appreciative noises, but my sense of taste had entirely disappeared. I might have been eating empty gelatine capsules. The sense of taste was not the only one of my senses to be affected. Throughout the meal, I had the uncomfortable feeling that I was dually present: I was present to watch myself performing all the animal movements, the social activities required of sharing a meal, but I was observing from the outside. I had no perception of the feelings of the activities; I was simply observing them, a naturalist quietly noting the behaviours of a social group of primates, but with no idea of how the food tasted or what the sounds and gestures meant to them. I don't know how my conscious brain responded to questions or stories. I couldn't hear them. I could only observe myself participating.

We were all drinking Kevin's flowery, watery elderberry wine, and gradually, in some peculiar inversion of nature, the alcohol began restoring feeling to my body and sense to my brain. I began to hear the stories of the lives of Fiona and Kevin and found myself appreciating the meaning of words again. Kevin began recounting his experiences with his most intriguing guests in a seemingly unending recitation of the gentle lunacy of gentle people and I laughed again. I looked at Sabasa and saw her smiling sadly at me. I lifted my goblet of elderberry wine and smiled in return. She blushed and looked down briefly and then took one of Fiona's hands in hers and smiled at me again. My smile was my benison. I was no longer hollow, but I was no longer the person I had briefly been.

The lunch continued through the afternoon until Sabasa suddenly turned to me and said, "I can't stand it anymore. I have to cut your hair, Thom!"

"That would be a relief," I answered.

Fiona went out to fetch a pair of scissors and a comb, Kevin found a bedsheet to drape around me, and Sabasa stood behind me, fussing her fingers through my hair and muttering about what was to be done.

When the scissors returned, Sabasa set to work, stopping only to step back, consider her work, laugh at the result, and return to the fray.

"It's not really..." Fiona began uncertainly.

Sabasa laughed. "No, it's really not, is it?"

Kevin, still helping himself to his wine began sniggering helplessly.

"Well, great. Thanks ladies," I offered peevishly.

"No, no," Sabasa assured me hurriedly. "It'll be all right, I promise."

I didn't care. I wanted to feel her hands on my head, touching my scalp, pulling and fussing with my hair. I didn't care if she shaved it all off—as long as it took forever. Samson never enjoyed a haircut more.

Finally, Sabasa stepped back from her handiwork, unpeeled the bed sheet from around my neck and carefully shook the trimmings onto the floor. Kevin began sweeping it into a pile, telling us how good hair was for the compost. Fiona smiled at me, proud of the job her Claire had done.

Sabasa held up the hand mirror for me to admire her work.

"Well, it's different," I began, "and thank Christ for that!"

Sabasa beamed with delight. In truth, it wasn't much of a haircut and only an improvement because the original was so dire, but it was an improvement, and it did make me look a different person. I would need that.

I cannot now remember much about the afternoon and evening. We spent it talking, helping Kevin with jobs around the ashram, preparing a simple soup for dinner. I became used to seeing Sabasa and Fiona as a couple, even though, following the strict policy of physical abstinence that Kevin insisted on as part of the spiritual therapy, there was no overt touching or caressing. The effort they took not to betray their feelings made their attraction and longing for each other invincibly charming. They looked like schoolgirls with a crush on each other; an accidental brushing hands as they helped prepare the meal would cause one to blush, the other to smile or flick water from the basin on the other or some other playful teasing. Strangely, I felt no jealousy or anger. I only felt loss. It was probably a helpful introduction.

I went to bed early, feigning tiredness and exaggerating the effects of my virus to cover the emotional exhaustion I was suffering. I lay in my pod as the darkness deepened around me. I might have been buried in the rubble of a temple or the dirt of a backyard. I thought of the childish message I had left on the underside of the slab of concrete covering Crennan. I was buried more darkly than he ever would be. The darkness continued to fall over me, handful by handful.

Return

> Long day at the ashram. Flew back from Hobart. Still not well. Sabasa and Fiona should be heading to Ulverstone. Should call Kevin in a few days to see if he needs cash and to promise to head back sometime. Knitting up more ravelled sleeves than I knew I had.

When I'd bought my ticket to Tasmania, I had half-hoped I would be pressed by Sabasa to stay longer and fully-hoped that we would return together. As those dreams had been meticulously dissected, pinned, and displayed for examination and found to be nothing but a commonplace, not a rare butterfly but a cabbage moth, I was now pleased to have an excuse to leave. I slept, or pretended to sleep, for as long as possible the next morning. It saved a couple of hours, but the day still dragged. Everyone was affected by my mood, I think. Kevin found new interest in meditating alone, and Sabasa and Fiona were quiet and sad. The previous day's girlishness seemed to have left them entirely. I presume they had discussed Claire's absurd, old roué and found him so pathetic that they couldn't laugh at him; they could only feel sorry for him. I embarrassed them.

Kevin tried to rally us with a consciousness-clearing session in the afternoon, but we stroked the Tibetan singing bowls flaccidly and arrhythmically, and never managed to achieve the harmonious ringing vibration that Kevin had promised us. He led us in some of his idiosyncratic chants, but even his unquenchable optimism was tested when his gong broke free of its polished babul frame and rolled off the table, clattering, misshapen and out of tune, to the floor. He spoke of the need to cleanse the negative energy and suggested we all retreat to our pods for silent contemplation while he burnt sage and frankincense to reinvigorate the space. We retired thankfully.

Towards evening, Sabasa and Fiona drove me to the airport, both making half-hearted attempts to make me stay a few more days. Sabasa had planned to leave the ashram later in the week, but she had nothing left in Melbourne she wanted to collect; so she had decided to stay with Fiona at her place in Ulverstone and to help in her café and crafts shop opposite the Historical Museum. It promised to be a life of slow, genteel poverty—a little like the life I had thought to offer her, but without the Spanish cooking and language lessons and heterosexual companionship.

I convinced them not to wait for my departure at the airport and we said our awkward goodbyes, complete with wholly unsatisfactory hugs, on the forecourt. We made all the expected promises of keeping in touch, of visiting, of catching up regularly, of meeting again at the ashram. Sabasa and Fiona drove away, Sabasa leaning out the window, waving, smiling, and blowing kisses. I stood watching them, waving and trying to smile.

Back in Melbourne, back at home, I took to bed. I tried to remember what my routine had been before the Spanish incursion, but I could hardly remember how I had filled my days. I must have slept for twenty hours of each twenty-four for the next couple of days. True, I was still enveloped in a viral fug which hampered my thinking, but even when moments of clarity threatened, I found myself seeing Sabasa's face, worried, sorrowful, loving, as she asked, "You didn't think...?" And I didn't. I couldn't. I simply fell asleep again.

Slowly, the mechanical necessities of living reasserted themselves and I began to move, shuffling around the house in an approximation of a living being. I started eating again. I had several pots of tea each day. I began blinking into consciousness again. My recovery coincided with the first suspicions of optimism creeping back into my thinking. Sabasa had discovered love with Fiona because Fiona's was an even safer love than mine. But would that safety satisfy her?

Couldn't this be a classic case of a rebound relationship? Was there no chance that Sabasa might yet appear on my doorstep, hoping to share what I offered: freedom, choice, mutual respect? Didn't those people who fell in with controlling partners almost invariably place themselves back in similar situations? I began to look for evidence of Fiona's controlling nature. I couldn't find it, which I managed to twist into support for the view that that's how their relationship would unfold. After all, weren't controlling people, by their nature, expert at disguising it?

The fantasy of a future life with Sabasa was too appealing to abandon. I indulged myself in daydreams of its realisation. It may have been a stupid, adolescent behaviour, but it helped me recover an ability to function in daily life. Days passed, but order reasserted itself. I remembered to put the rubbish out. I thinned the pond weed in Norma's pond. I vacuumed the house, remembering to think of the main bedroom as "Norma's bedroom", not "Sabasa's". My dreams of a possible future with Sabasa, whatever that future might hold, gave me purpose. I even recovered sufficiently to try to add something to my political reformation project.

*

Why we need a constitution and why it needs a 'why'

Extract from A Programme of Moderate Political Reform in Australia, www.pmpra.com

The Australian Constitution is a peculiar document. Purportedly the "set of rules by which a country or state is run"[10], it is actually the set of rules to administer existing rules or to make new ones. The constitution sets out the mechanism of how the country is run and how the laws of the country may be made or altered. There's not much else to it.

---

[10] See "Closer Look — The Australian Constitution" published by the Parliamentary Education Office, undated.

It is a dreary document. It focuses on the *'how'* of running the country, without ever exploring the *'why'*.

Why does Australia exist? Why should it exist? I contend that if we don't have an agreed 'why' we can never have a meaningful 'how'. After all, I can develop the perfect technique to bowl leg spin—the 'how'—but without the game of cricket, without the reason of trying to get a batsman out, what is the point? You need the 'why'.

It is historically understandable that we have this elaborate 'how' of a constitution: that was the urgent need of the day. It was never the important need of the day. It was urgent, because with six separate colonies, all keen to promote their separate interests first and their common interests second, the mechanism of government seemed the most critical problem to agree. This was also a time when 'why' hardly qualified as a interrogative adverb: Queen Victoria ruled an empire so self-assuredly complacent that its ideals were universal ideals, its practices the acme of human endeavour, its institutions the measure against which all social institutions should be measured, that the question of 'why' must have been unthinkable. This was an empire which could stumble onto an intriguingly complex continent, populated with a rich and diverse set of cultures, and declare it empty.

But just because the administrators and functionaries of a long-gone empire were obsessed with how and not why, does not mean we should never consider it. The constitution should make the case for why Australia should exist at all. What are our ideals? Why do we want to exist? What do we hope to achieve? It is only when we have our immediate answers to these fundamental, these truly existential questions, that we can hope to govern ourselves towards the objectives those answers provide. Without them, we are without determined direction. We are drifting at the pleasure of wind, tide, and whim. Our current constitution gives us the rudder, the mechanism to steer by, but we have no charts, no sailing directions, no planned ports-of-call, no hoped-for destination.

We must rewrite our constitution to include the reasons Australia should exist. If these reasons are not noble enough, are not laudable, are not inspiring enough that we, her citizens, would not stand behind them, accepting them as personal goals, accepting both the effort and sacrifice we might need to achieve them, we should accept that Australia has no point, no purpose in existing.

Return

*

On the appointed day of my final visit to Dr No, I woke feeling as though the worst had passed. Physically, I felt weak, but normal. My knee was still bruised and still tender if prodded, but it was no trouble when I stood or walked. I toyed with the idea of cancelling the appointment, but my newly awakened sense of normalcy and the need to re-establish order in my life convinced me to keep the appointment. Male optimism was reasserting its reassuring control over my thinking. I reported to the receptionist and sat in the waiting room. Dr No did not appear to call me in. His receptionist took a call and then instructed me to go in. It was unusual. It was unsettling not to hear his brusque, clipped order to attention and forward march to the consultation. I was flustered.

Doctor No says... nothing much

> I do not need antibiotics. I need to vomit.

I knocked at Dr No's room and entered. He was seated at his desk. He motioned me to the examination table without looking up.

"Trousers off. We will examine your knee."

I slouched over to the examination table, undid my belt, and let my trousers fall to my ankles. I sat on the examination table and waited. Dr No completed his notes for his last patient and opened my folder. He looked at me, unblinking and tapped the folder.

"I have been reviewing your notes, Mr Furphy. Very interesting.

"Oh?" I questioned weakly.

"Yes," he said, standing and walking around his desk to stand in front of me. "Medically tedious. Socially interesting."

Before I could make any reply, he turned his attention to my knee.

"Still sore to walk?" he asked, gently prodding the bruise.

"No, no. It's fine now. Bit stiff for a few days, but right as rain now."

"And erections? Are we still concerned?"

"I think... I don't think we need to explore that any more," I spluttered. The idea of talking to Dr No about erections was somehow more chilling than never having another.

Dr No nodded slowly, withdrawing his stethoscope from his lab coat pocket.

"Shirt off," he commanded, and then listened to my chest while instructing me to breathe in, out, hold it, and so on.

He snapped the stethoscope out of his ears and let it hang around his neck.

"Clear enough. No need for antibiotics."

"Good."

Dr No turned and walked back to his desk, sitting down and jotting a couple of notes in my folder. I began doing up my shirt and pulling up my trousers.

"Now, Mr Furphy, a couple more questions for you. You do not need to answer."

I stopped, not knowing what to expect. I had threaded the tongue of my belt through its buckle, but stood frozen while I waited. He paused, as if considering how to put his questions.

"I am a liar, Mr Furphy."

It was not the opening I expected.

"How do you mean, Dr No?" Was he perhaps about to confess that he wasn't a doctor? It wouldn't have worried me.

"I am a liar. Just like you, Mr Furphy. But I am a good liar and you are not."

"Liar?" It was all I could manage.

"Yes, when necessary, I lie to my patients. I lied to you."

"I'm not following you, doctor."

"Yes, you are following, Mr Furphy, you simply don't understand. I lied to you about the bruise on your knee. I have never see a mark like that; certainly, I have never seen a face bruised by the trigger of a gun, but the mark on your knee did resemble a trigger."

I waited. He might have wanted me to commit myself to speech, but I was so unsure of where Dr No was heading with this that I retreated to my preferred court room defence: silence.

"And yet, interesting that when I told you it was made by a gun, you did not attempt to deny it. In fact, you confirmed it: a toy gun, you said."

"Yes, my nephews…"

"Nephews? Good! I want to talk to you about this family I am learning about now."

"Well, I don't see how it matters…" I began, but Dr No cut me off.

"Mr Furphy. Please. You are a bad liar. You have no nephews. There was no toy gun. Clearly, there was a gun. You have admitted as much."

"Not in so many words," I offered. Dr No didn't even waste a disparaging look on me. His eyes were fixed on me. He looked cold and he looked dangerous.

"I do not like guns, Mr Furphy. I particularly do not like guns when idiots and liars are involved. And I become very curious about idiots and liars and guns when a man with no family and no medicare card turns out to live at the same address as an old patient of mine."

Dr No waited and I waited with him. I broke first.

"Norma was my auntie."

Dr No nodded slowly, never taking his eyes of me.

"Norma was not your auntie or anyone's auntie. She was my patient for over two decades. She was a patient of this practice for many decades before that. I know her history. She has no family. She lives in her parents' house; the same house in which she was born. She has not come into the practice for over three years. And now, you live at the same address."

"Norma was my aunt. We all called her aunt but she may really be some sort of cousin of my mother's. I moved in to care for her, but about eighteen months ago, she had to be moved first to respite care and then her family—she has family in Sydney—

moved her to a nursing home in Sydney so she could be near them. I'm living in the house to keep it maintained."

Dr No paused again, then began speaking quietly as he made notes.

"Some sort of cousin of MY mother... HER family moved her... SHE has family in Sydney."

He looked at me.

"Mr Furphy, your words betray you because you are a bad liar. You say she's a cousin of your mother's, but you don't refer to 'my' family or 'our' family, you say 'her' family: '*her* family moved her... *she* has family in Sydney'."

I shrugged at this flimsy, linguistic bluster. Dr No pressed on.

"You say she was moved to respite care and then to a nursing home."

"Yes, because she was."

He nodded slowly.

"How odd. How odd that neither the respite care facility nor the nursing home should be interested in Norma's medical records."

I felt my stomach empty itself into my intestines. Dr No continued his quiet dissection.

"I have patients every year who move to nursing homes, retirement villages, go to live with relatives interstate. I know when they have left because always, *always*, Mr Furphy, another practice or specialist will require their notes. People do not require *less* medical care as they age."

He looked at me coldly.

"After I became interested in that bruise on your knee, Mr Furphy, which you confirmed was caused by a gun, and I awoke to the fact that you were living in Norma's house, I requested a search for a death certificate for her."

I stood staring blankly at him. I still hadn't fastened my belt. I lowered my gaze from his and began to fix my belt and trousers.

"There is no death certificate because she's been moved to Sydney," I blurted out.

"Perhaps you could tell me the name of the nursing home, then? I will contact them and find out who is currently looking after her medical needs so I can send her notes."

"I… I don't have it on me. Rosewood? Or Rose something. I'll call you with their details tomorrow," I offered, bending down now to tie my shoes. I wanted nothing more than to get out of his office and work out what to do.

"Tomorrow? Try to call me this afternoon, Mr Furphy. It won't be difficult for you, surely?"

"Fine. This afternoon. Not a problem. But there's really nothing to fuss about."

"Pay reception on your way out, Mr Furphy. I will expect a call this afternoon. I don't want to have to initiate further enquiries unless I have to. I dislike dealing with the police as much as I dislike guns."

*

Optimism—the male inheritance

Extract from the unpublished work, 'Masculinear', by Thomas Furphy

Men are biologically inclined to optimism. This is an essential requirement for the reasoning, but expendable, organism. If we accept that the male role is to protect, to fight, to gain biological advantage, in short, to be expendable, then the species needs to protect itself from a gender which might shirk those responsibilities in the face of extreme danger. While the male capacity for reasoning is not widely or extensively developed, it does exist. There will, therefore, be occasions when men—the gender elected to protect— might be faced with such overwhelming odds that reason would dictate that they turn tail and flee. Strangely, they tend not to. It is misnamed bravery, but it is not. It is the biological imperative of optimism.

Doctor No says... nothing much

Of course, you are now thinking of all those famous military routs, of those shameful times when men have thrown down their weapons and run, but—and this is the important point—usually only *after* they have faced certain defeat and certain defeat is undeniably upon them. It is rare for men to have enough foresight to begin packing up and moving out in time to avoid slaughter, even when reason would suggest that slaughter is the most likely outcome.

Why? Why can we list dozens of instances of heroic[11], but inevitable, failure in the face of overwhelming odds? Why, even in those instances of disgraceful abandoning of posts, did men allow themselves to be at those posts in the first place?

Optimism.

Nature has thoughtfully provided men with a capacity for optimism which is engaged by the male brain in inverse proportion to the likely outcome. This optimism is expressed in many ways—"It'll probably be all right", "The men at the top know what they're doing", "God is with us", "We've got through worse before", "What have we got to lose?", "She will probably come back to me", and so on and so on; ten thousand comforting platitudes, all with one thing in common: they fly in the face of reason.

Optimism allows us to face annihilation and to be annihilated. That's what we are designed for.

*

I scurried back to Norma's house, not thinking anything, but knowing I had to hurry. It was only as I stepped inside the front gate, as I looked up at my beautiful, comforting, solid, red-brick home, as I saw the rose bushes which lined the low, brick wall, that I realised I had lost everything. One can fall in love with things, with places, as readily as with people. I loved this house and the things it contained.

There are moments which cannot be confined to time. They are so densely packed with significance that they exist outside time. I saw the whole. I saw everything. I saw the roses and

---

[11] Any female readers left at this advanced point in the book may like to substitute 'stupid' for 'heroic'.

realised I would never prune them, never dead head them again. I saw the house which had sheltered Norma and me and realised I had lost it. I saw the contents of Norma's house: the crockery, the pictures on the walls, the writing table, the telephone seat. I saw the sanctuary of the backyard, the beautiful pond I had created for Norma, the slightly shabby garage which housed Betsy. I saw I had lost my connection to the woman whose life I had undertaken to chronicle. I had lost the haven where, for the only time in my life, I had been able to work and live and thrive. I had lost the connection to the history of the contents of the house. I had lost the centre of the life I still had hoped to share with Sabasa. I had lost all the love I had known, all the love I had imagined, all the love I had promised.

When I realised Sabasa loved another, I had been crushed. I had known how Crennan had been crushed. Now I knew how it was to die. Everything left me. I had no breath. I had no thought beyond the experience of the moment. I had no body. I had no life. I understood everything and everything had ended.

Metamorphosis

> *I cannot continue writing as Crennan. End.*

Death is rapid when it comes. I stepped into the house and knew that Thomas Furphy had ended. I had to leave the house immediately and resume life as I had known it before. I would have to gather my old backpack and those few possessions I could carry with me. It overwhelmed me. The house and its contents were precious to me. Could I leave behind Norma's Royal Doulton Pansies teapot, creamer, and sugar bowl? Her writing desk? The framed blueprint of Norman Selfe's prize-winning Sydney Harbour Bridge design? Her bone handled carving set? The set of souvenir teaspoons? It was impossible to consider life without the genteel refinement that Norma had brought into my life.

I had no choice. Life is a dream and we always awaken. I had to leave the house and everything in it before Dr No let slip the hounds of law.

It was thinking about No that brought me back to my senses. I realized with a curious pang that Dr No didn't like me, had never liked me. I had always thought of him as a comical, generous man. I had always thought there was some secret sympathy between us. I had always assumed that beneath the curt, gruff exterior, Dr No rather liked me, that we shared an anarchical understanding of the world. I now could see that he didn't like me and never had. I also knew that once No decided on an action, he would take it, and I further knew that I was no match for him. No would satisfy himself that the law found out what had happened to his patient or they would answer to him.

I had to get out.

I began thinking clearly again. I had no shortage of money. I had access to two identities, three if you counted the power of attorney for Norma. As I assembled a practical assortment of possessions for an experienced urban homesteader, my plans began to form. I realized with disgust that I would have to become Crennan: no one would be looking too hard for him and as long as I remained hidden in the urban wild, no one would find him. I was likely to have access to Norma's bank accounts for a long time. While there was no one to inherit her estate, there would be no one screaming to have access to her accounts. It would take months, possibly years, for anyone to stop the dividends arriving into her account. Perhaps they never would. I also had access to Crennan's bank account and although this would dry up soon enough, I could probably bank on the Victorian Police continuing to pay his salary until he was eventually dismissed. Three months? Six months?

I packed sensible clothes. I slipped my laptop into the pack—I still needed to write, even if my work patterns would return to the patchy, chance occasions an urban homesteading life affords. I packed my spirit stove and camping pans, rolled oats, tea, aluminium foil, duct tape, nylon cord, and garbage bags[12]. I rolled a nylon quilt in a long sausage around the backpack and tied it securely around the pack. I began cleaning the house of all my possessions, leaving Norma's neatly in place, just as she had always left them. I packed the stack of my excess possessions into several garbage bags and loaded them into Betsy. I then made one final run in Norma's car to a bank of charity bins and deposited the detritus of Thomas Furphy within them. I parked Betsy back in the garage, slipped the key under the mat, and locked the garage for the last time.

By mid-afternoon, Thomas Furphy boarded a Qantas flight to Adelaide where Scott Crennan met the flight just over an hour later.

---

[12] Basic urban homesteading kit.

Adelaide

*

The first task

Extract from the unpublished work, 'Urban Homesteading—Surviving in the Urban Wild', by Scott Crennan

The first consideration of any day is to determine where you will sleep that night. Any preparation for that task must be completed before anything else. Once you have a plan for the night ahead, any secondary tasks can be considered: food, clothing, washing.

The reason for making this your first task is that it is the most difficult and is the only one that directly affects your safety. You can live for weeks without food. You can survive without washing. Where you sleep, however, directly affects whether you wake up. There are three considerations when selecting a sleeping place: security, dryness/warmth, comfort. Security, your safety, must always come first.

*

A new city is a formidable challenge. You do not realise how much you know about a city until you leave it and attempt to be as comfortable in the new as you were in the old. Even before I had a house in Melbourne, I had knowledge of dozens of places I could shower, wash clothes, find toilets, and at least as many nooks where one could doss for the night, dry and safe. I also had half a dozen places I could use to stash small packs of possessions safely. In Adelaide, I had knowledge of none.

I stepped out of the airport and into a cold, Adelaide evening. It wasn't raining, but it felt as though it might. Those who are new to sleeping out invariably look to the wrong places to sleep. They head for the inner city, or look around train lines or train stations, or try to find shelter in a park. These are all bad choices. All cities have a secondary population, a population that only emerges in the night. Most of this population should be avoided, particularly when you are wearing your 'New In

Town' t-shirt. The best way to avoid this population is to look for a reasonably well-heeled suburb, one which is unused to having nocturnal campers. In a middle-class suburb there are always plenty of safe places in which to sleep and, if worse comes to worst, you can sleep openly on the verandah of one of the houses. As long as you're quiet and only settle down after the lights are out, you can be assured of a safe night's sleep. If you happen to snore too loudly, an outraged householder may accost you and send you on your way, but they won't attack you. Sometimes they feed you.

I had used the airport WIFI to do a little research and knew which suburbs I should be looking in to find a safe place to doss down. I had money, of course, and could have spent a night or two in a hotel, but that way lies ruin for the urban homesteader. I needed to conserve money and I needed to start learning my way around Adelaide as soon as possible.

I bought a ticket for the buses that would last for the rest of the day, took a bus into the city and then headed south towards Kingswood and Torrens, two of the suburbs which seemed likely to provide me shelter. I found what I was looking for in Highgate, even closer to the city: a sixties, cream brick block of walk-up flats. These almost always have a common laundry or utility room at the back of the block on the ground floor, but these days everyone has their own washing machine and is far too precious to use communal facilities; so these rooms are usually empty and insecurely locked if locked at all. I walked around the back of these flats and found the expected laundry/utility room. It was clearly not in use anymore. A feeble-looking wire hasp and staple was locked with a small padlock, but the hasp fixture had simply been screwed into the door. I expect the padlock had never been opened after it had been fitted and doubted anyone could have located the key. I could easily have pulled out the hasp, but in the interests of building my store of hiding places, I elected to return later that night with a screwdriver and let myself in discreetly.

Adelaide

I left my block of flats and returned to the main road and caught a bus back towards the city. My plan was to find a large supermarket with a hardware section, buy a screwdriver and a padlock, and to return to the flats late at night, effect my entry, and, presuming everything was quiet, fix the new lock so I could secure the space as my own.

Ordinarily, by which I mean, 'in the days before I moved into Norma's house', the finding and securing of a new bolt hole caused me some rejoicing. It is no small thing to find you have secured, even temporarily, a piece of real estate for the cost of a padlock and screwdriver. Today, however, I was strangely unresponsive. I was purposeless. I felt that I was observing the rituals of my kind, but without hope or purpose, an atheist priest swinging the censer and intoning the words, but empty. Like a priest, I knew no other way of providing for myself; so I observed the form, but it brought me no joy, no hope, no purpose.

Despite appearances, Adelaide is not too staid a city to have late night shopping, and I found a camping store where I bought the requisite supplies. I also thought to buy a groundsheet and a cheap air mattress. I still had several hours before I could assume the good burghers of Highgate would be settled in front of their televisions or making their final cups of cocoa for the night and wouldn't notice any unusual sounds coming from the communal laundry. Lugging my purchases and still wearing my backpack, I went looking for a budget restaurant that was used to serving heavily laden backpackers. I very rarely buy meals—I am adept at foraging in supermarkets—but tonight was an occasion. Becoming Scott Crennan was a trencher of self-loathing that I would have to choke down, but I needed something else in my stomach if I was to be able to stand it.

Although Adelaide is a capital city and its marketing people would have you believe it is full of great restaurants (to match its great late night shopping!), on a weekday night after

8:00 PM, options for a simple meal are limited. I found a struggling chop house just off Rundle Mall. It didn't look clean or comfortable and it wasn't well patronised, but it stayed open until midnight. It had the one desirable quality I was looking for: the tired woman who reheated and served the food was never going to throw anyone out if they had ordered a meal and then spent a couple of hours nursing a coffee. Perfect. I ordered a Malaysian Chicken Curry with vegetables and rice and ate the grey chicken stew which arrived. It was plentiful.

I stayed in the restaurant until around 11:30 and then headed back to my flats. There were lights on in a couple of the flats, but it was quiet. The back of the block of flats was dimly lit by one security light. I regretted not having bought a torch, which would have made it easier to remove and refit the hasp and staple, but it made little difference in the end. Unscrewing the hasp from the door took less than a minute. I left the hasp and padlock hanging on the door jamb. I would either fit my new lock tomorrow or reassemble the original fitting to disguise my occupation of the room. I pushed the door open and stepped inside. Again, I regretted not having a torch, but I could see a light switch by the side of the door and decided that, once the door was shut, turning on the light would be less suspicious than the sight of a torch beam flicking around.

The thin, yellow light of the bare bulb which the switch surprised into life revealed that the room had indeed once been a laundry. There was a pair of concrete troughs fastened against one wall, each tub with a brass tap hanging off the exposed pipes above it. In one corner, an old Flatley clothes dryer trailed a frayed electric cord. There wasn't much else. The room was decorated with a grimy sprinkling of domestic detritus: broken clothes horse, wire racks from a refrigerator, a couple of kitchen chairs. And dust. Gritty, slightly greasy dust underfoot. The nicotine yellow lino was coated in the dust of neglect and the glacial progress of decay. It was dispiriting.

Adelaide

I put the shopping bag down and surveyed the space again. I moved a chair against the door to hold it shut in the night. I tried one of the taps and a brown trickle of sludge gradually cleared to allow clean water to flow. That was good. I had water. I also had somewhere to urinate if I needed to. I had power for the lights and the Flatley suggested that there was at least one powerpoint in the room; so I should be able to charge my laptop and, if I made another trip to the camping store, I could buy an electric jug or small hotplate. As temporary living quarters, it was close to what I would once have thought of as ideal, but Norma's house had changed my definition of ideal.

There was enough clear floor space in front of the tubs to spread out my groundsheet and unpack the air mattress. I knelt on the groundsheet and blew up the air mattress, growing dizzy as it inflated. I untied and unrolled the quilt from around my pack. Then I stood unsteadily, switched off the light, stepped carefully back to the groundsheet, took off my shoes, and wriggled onto the air mattress and under the quilt.

I lay in the darkness. I thought of nothing. I fell asleep.

I woke in the early hours of the morning with an overwhelming feeling of misery: deep, existential misery. There was just enough light in the room to allow me to pick out the contents of the laundry. It wasn't just my situation in the laundry, I realised. I was cold. The misery I was feeling began to resolve itself into its component parts: the mattress had deflated in the night and I was now lying on the cold, hard linoleum floor and I had a terrible pain in my stomach and bowels.

Consciousness returned in a dense wave of nausea. I realised I was very, very sick. I pulled myself upright and my mouth filled with saliva. My stomach was churning with the urgency of an advanced case of food poisoning. I rolled to one side and started to stand up and as I did so I could feel an extraordinary pressure in my bowel. I clenched my sphincter shut but knew that whatever was in there was about to be expelled. I hurried

Adelaide

over to the concrete laundry tubs. It was all I could do. I dropped my trousers, clawed my underpants down, spun around so my arse was back against the laundry basin, and, placing my hands on the rim, I hopped and lifted myself up onto the cold, metal rim of a trough, my arse hanging into the tub. I was just in time. A jet of liquid shit was propelled out of my arse and into the tub. I could feel it splatter over my buttocks. The room was filled with the stench of raw shit and barely digested Malaysian Chicken Curry. It was disgusting. I realised I had only begun the purge. My stomach now revolted against the smell. I leaned over the companion tub and vomited, painfully and fully. I could smell coffee. I wondered how the chicken curry had found its way through my gut and the coffee had remained in my stomach. My wondering ceased as a second spasm caused my lower bowel to remember its function and another liquid jet of shit gushed out.

I was simultaneously hot and cold. I spat into the second tub to try to clear the vomit from my mouth. I was panting. The smell of the shit, bile, vomit, curry, and coffee was overpowering. I turned on the tap above the vomit tub with the thought of trying to wash it down, but my effort to turn while perched on the rim of the concrete tubs was too much for one of the rusted bolts holding one side of the tubs to the wall. It sheared off. The set of tubs lurched under me. I tried to lean back against the wall to correct for the weight of the slumping tubs, but the sudden movement of throwing my body back caused all the bolts to fail. The concrete tubs were torn off the wall and I pitched forward onto the quilt and deflated mattress, the basins emptying their vile contents over me, the quilt, the groundsheet, over everything. The concrete troughs landed on the back of my knees, smashing the patella of one and dislocating the other. The tap continued running, diluting my misery until it began flowing beneath the chair, under the door, and out into the Adelaide morning. Through a stinking cloud of agony, cold and wet, I noted that my morning erections were as persistently absent as ever.

Epilogue

This packet of papers was sent to the ashram about eighteen months after the visit of Claire, Fiona, and Thom described in it. There was no letter or other instructions. I kept them thinking that Thom (or Scott, as he now seems to be calling himself) would turn up for them, but after a year of no contact, I tried calling and emailing him, but received no response.

I am publishing them now in the hope that Thom might see them and get in touch, if only to pick up any royalties which might accrue, or someone who knows him or recognises him from this story might direct him to contact me. I will be holding any monies raised by publication in the ashram account but I openly acknowledge that any of the profits must go to Thom if he can be found.

I have not altered the text of the papers in any way, indeed, the condition of the text (one or two inconsistencies excepted) suggested to me that Thom had prepared them for publication, and this featured in my decision to publish them. I think it was his intention that I should.

I have said that I haven't altered the text at all, and this is perhaps a little surprising given the sometimes unflattering way the Enlightenment Centre and I are portrayed; so I hope I will be forgiven for adding a very short piece by way of correction about the Centre and allowed also to add a few salient points about the characters in these papers as I knew them.

First, Thom's descriptions of people that I met are largely accurate. I think his characterisation of Claire tends too much to her physical charms and neglects her intellect and radiant spirituality. To those sensitive to auras, Claire has a very powerful electromagnetic aura which manifests as a shimmering orange and pink aura with flashes of blue when she is engaged in thought or remembrance. Her friend, Fiona, was similar, but with greens and reds predominating. She was at once both energising and calming. If Thom is to be believed and Claire and Fiona were attracted to each other, I would not discount the possibility that this was a spiritual, rather than physical attraction. They were both very attractive souls. They certainly expressed an intention to live and work together in Ulverstone in Fiona's business and I would predict success for such a powerful and attractive pair.

Thom's description of me is, I think, affectionate, but is not accurate. I have a very clear spiritual philosophy which is anything but a hotch potch of world religions, or whatever expression he used. It is a single path which anyone may take and attain a state of enlightenment. Part of the difficulty, I think, that Thom has with my philosophy is his inability to accept that a 'state of enlightenment' is not the same thing from one spiritual being to another. Therefore, when chanting with Thom, for example, he might claim to be unmoved, but the act of being unmoved, his unmoveableness being manifest, is itself evidence of a state of enlightenment. Light is a spectrum, after all. Thom was never able to accept that he had already reached several moments of enspectrumment, if you will.

Thom makes mention of my intention to document my philosophy more fully and I intend to have completed the first volume of this work early next year. Anyone interested in learning more is invited to contact me at the ashram. Contact details follow.

The description of the ashram is faithful, although I have now added a bath house and massage chamber, and two of the hives now include double beds. Thom is incorrect when he says I have 'rules' prohibiting sexual congress. Expressing one's spiritual needs or gifts through the beautiful and satisfying medium of respectful sexual activity is to be encouraged and enjoyed by all. I only caution visitors to the ashram to beware of material sex, which is the sexual activity commonly practised in our society. Until visitors are confident that they

Epilogue

can recognise the distinction, I urge them to refrain from sex in order that, when they resume sexual activity, they will do so with a mind attuned to the spiritual plane and when that happens, they will experience sex in a way that they have never experienced it before. Far from prohibiting sex, one of the services I offer is that of sexual coach, assisting couples or singles to open themselves to sexual acts that arouse the spirit as well as the body.

The picture of Thom in these papers is also not accurate, in my opinion. Thom is more thoughtful and considerate that he suggests. Far from being a sceptical cynic, he was instrumental in the establishment of the ashram. He worked with me for several months without reward and I think he is as proud as I am of what it has become. As for some of the more remarkable actions he confesses to have undertaken, I am quite convinced that he would be *capable* of such things, but that is not the same thing as believing he has done them. When I saw him at the ashram with Claire and Fiona, for example, he did not look like a man who had recently murdered another. I allow myself to be a pretty fair judge of these sorts of things. Murder leaves the aura cloudy, a murky, dark grey, and I never saw this in Thom's. Even his claim to have fallen in love with Claire is something I hold improbable. His behaviour was not of a man smitten or hopelessly in love, but rather a man who loved her as he loved me and as I love him. He was fond of her, no doubt, but no more than fond than we all should be of all other men and women, all other living beings. I may be misjudging him, but that's my assessment. I look forward to seeing him again at the ashram.

Anyone who has contact with Thom might also like to tell him there is another reason for visiting me. I am holding a letter addressed to him from Claire which arrived for him a few months before his packet of papers. There is no sender's address on the envelope, just his pet name for her, Sabasa, and it is postmarked Sydney, not Ulverstone. I thought about opening it and appending its contents to these papers, but decided against it. Thom will know that he can collect if from me or have me forward it if he'd like.

Finally, I would like to add a word or two about the work of the Enlightenment Centre. The purpose of the Lotus Enlightenment Centre is to allow people to accept transformation in their lives. We offer a supportive environment in which you can renew or reimagine yourself and the life you choose to live.

The Centre is a spiritual retreat, but it is not a hiding place. Spiritual retreat is not a withdrawal or acceptance of defeat, but a renewing of your life path. Our Centre is managed by me, and I willingly share my life experience and wisdom freely with all who attend and study. We offer the opportunity to study meditation and chanting routines to further the spiritual learning experience. We concentrate on providing all attendees, whatever their background and no matter how advanced on their paths, with a pure atmosphere, surrounded by like-minded people who radiate inner peace and a connection with the source of all understanding and life.

The Centre is a haven of tranquillity and growth. We offer special courses in non-judgemental conflict resolution, positive non-oppositional perception awareness raising, and corporate team building and team maintaining training. We have a special course for business, government, and corporate customers: Understanding and Embracing Otherness while Respecting our Ourness. We are acknowledged experts in corporate culture realignment and repair and offer a particularly supportive environment for managers and team members who may be in conflict or who fear future conflicts in the workplace.

We provide delicious Vegan vegetarian meals and welcome the involvement of guests in designing or creating the meals.

A visit to the Lotus Enlightenment Centre offers the priceless value of spiritual refreshment for a modest material fee. Long or short stays are welcomed. Special rates for weekends.

Epilogue

Special rates for groups. Returning guests are always especially welcome and enjoy an additional discount in addition to any other discounts for which they may be eligible. Guests who are suffering financial hardship or who qualify as materially disadvantaged should contact me for a personal and confidential consultation to design a collaboratively agreed appropriate fee package.

For more information, or to book your stay with us, please contact Shushan on +61 3 6233 2229 or email lotusenlightenment@yandex.com.

www.ingramcontent.com/pod-product-compliance
Lightning Source LLC
Chambersburg PA
CBHW020254030426
42336CB00010B/761